D1030765

Power and Human Destiny

Power and Human Destiny

HERBERT ROSINSKI

Edited by Richard P. Stebbins

With a Foreword by

August Heckscher

FREDERICK A. PRAEGER, *Publishers*
New York · Washington · London

FREDERICK A. PRAEGER, *Publishers*
111 Fourth Avenue, New York 3, N.Y., U.S.A.
77–79 Charlotte Street, London W.1, England

Published in the United States of America in 1965
by Frederick A. Praeger, Inc., Publishers

Library of Congress Catalog Card Number: 65-15648

Printed in the United States of America

Foreword

HERBERT ROSINSKI was a man who seemed to carry about in him the seed of a major work. This book wanted to be the fulfillment awaited by many who knew him. He died while it was still going through successive drafts. To his friend Richard Stebbins we owe the orderliness and comparative completeness of the following pages— a labor which involved far more than that which usually falls to an editor, and which could have been accomplished only by one who was intimately familiar with the author's thought and was himself a practiced writer.

As the Director of The Twentieth Century Fund, I had been challenged by the possibility of helping Dr. Rosinski to make the contribution of which he seemed capable. In 1956, the Trustees made an appropriation allowing him time and scope for his efforts. He was no longer working with the Fund at the time of his death, and this brief introduction must be in the form of a quite personal expression of pleasure at seeing the book finally reach the public.

No one who reads these pages can fail to sense the steadiness of vision and the elevation of thought which Dr. Rosinski brought to his work. He aimed to see the past and the present in a single

perspective—to grasp entire the changes in man's lot and draw
out the lessons for our day. Because he saw things in the large
view, he could appraise the revolutions of the present epoch, not
minimizing their challenges or their consequences, but placing
them in the line of man's long development. As a race we had,
before this, met with profound transformations in human life,
and had managed to create new forms of social organization and
control. The revolutions of the twentieth century, Rosinski believed, were of an order of magnitude comparable to that which
first marked man's change from a wandering being sustained by
hunting to a rooted tiller of the soil. The race, as he saw it, is
still imperfectly equipped to meet such trials, intermittently rational and only in scattered ways able to transcend immediate
compulsions and necessities.

The concept of power which Rosinski used as a guiding thread
through the maze of history is one in need of fresh understanding.
Narrowed to its military or political implications, held to be
somehow at odds with man's better hopes and higher nature,
destined in the view of utopian democrats or Marxists to be ultimately transcended, power has fared poorly among contemporary
social philosophers. Rosinski made the concept central to his
view of man's future. Society itself has generated a vast power
which we cannot refuse to acknowledge and to exercise. Power
over nature is the central fact of modernity. This can lead to a
destruction of the natural world, to man's alienation from it, or
to some new balance between man and the large environment
of which he is a part. Our response to the challenge of power
will in the end mark the quality and determine the outcome of
our whole civilization.

The author's thinking developed from a preoccupation with
the military situation. When I first discussed this book with
him, it was largely in terms of power as it is currently used—a
factor in international policies and in problems of strategy. Indeed the earlier drafts carried the title "Power and Peace." The

more he worked on his material, the larger were the issues with which he felt compelled to deal. The experience was undoubtedly painful to him, as the creative process invariably is; it required a fusion of disciplines and a mastery of fresh knowledge. His work, as a consequence, moved slowly. His manuscript showed the strains of constant revision, and he was himself left dissatisfied and fatigued.

Herbert Rosinski had the sensitivity of a proud and ambitious man; but he was modest in accepting criticism and at the end ready, no matter what the costs to himself, to push on to a final formulation of his thinking. That so much has now reached publishable form is due to his capacity to inspire friendship and loyalty. No one who reads the following pages can doubt, I think, but that what many of us suspected of this man was true: He had within him the makings of a significant contribution to modern thinking. Even the gleams captured here cast a revealing light.

AUGUST HECKSCHER

Preface

THIS BOOK embodies the intellectual legacy of one of the most remarkable scholars and thinkers of our time. Writer, lecturer, and adviser to governments on three continents, Herbert Rosinski at the time of his death in 1962 was best known as an authority on international military questions, a leading interpreter of the work of General Carl von Clausewitz, and the author of a classic history of *The German Army* that did much to enlighten the English-speaking peoples about their principal antagonist in World War II. Less generally known was the fact that the military studies to which he owed his international reputation reflected only one segment of Dr. Rosinski's interests and capabilities. His real concern as a scholar encompassed the full sweep of human history and development, from its earliest beginnings down to and beyond the crisis of our own time. That wider subject, in essence, is what the present book is about.

To his reflections on the human experience Herbert Rosinski brought a historian's learning, a philosopher's disciplined insight, and the intellectual independence of a thorough individualist who had consistently remained aloof from the play of contemporary ideological fashions. From his examination of the development of military power, he had been led to an analysis of power itself, its role in the evolution of human societies, and its implications for the destiny of man. Like Hegel and Marx in the early decades of the last century, he found one of the central themes of history in man's continuing development of power and in the tendency of that power, once developed, to turn against its creator and create a new slavery—even, in the exaggerated conditions of our present era, to threaten his very survival. It was Rosinski's hope that a fresh examination of this perennial problem, drawing upon the accumulated experience of the past hundred years, would promote a better understanding of the role of power in human affairs and of the necessity of finding ways to reassert our control over it before we are destroyed or strangled by the works of our own hands.

A preoccupation with the problem of power requires no special justification at a time when almost every writer on public affairs feels called upon to deal with one or another aspect of that protean subject. What distinguishes Rosinski's analysis is primarily its breadth of historical perspective and its insistence on grappling not merely with one or more of the specialized forms of power— military, political, administrative, economic, and the like—but with the underlying reality of which he considered these to be merely the incidental expressions. His aim was neither to glorify power nor to disparage it, but simply to see it recognized for what it is and to indicate the kind of practical conclusions that must flow from this recognition.

In elaborating his theme the author drew freely on the work of earlier thinkers, from the Greeks to Hegel and from Marx to Teilhard de Chardin. The precise extent and limits of his indebtedness must, however, remain for others to assess. Among contemporary discussions of power, the one that most naturally invites comparison is Romano Guardini's brief but suggestive treatise, *Die Macht: Versuch einer Wegweisung* (1951). In spirit and tendency there is an unmistakable kinship between the reflections of the distinguished Catholic philosopher and those of the Protestant-trained but essentially unaffiliated author of *Power and Human Destiny*. Both writers take an extremely broad view of the nature of power; both reject the naïvely optimistic mentality that sees the growth of power as a built-in guarantee of peace and progress; both perceive that, on the contrary, the continued increase in power in the industrial era poses increasing dangers, and that its subjection to more effective control has become the essential task of our time. But where Guardini's attention focuses primarily on the moral questions involved in the exercise of power by men, Rosinski is concerned not only with these questions but also with the "objective" power exercised by men's creations, and with the ways in which these more recondite forms of power constrain and limit him. In essence, the two works are complementary rather than conflicting. Both exemplify the spirit of realistic and responsible analysis in which their authors see our only hope of meeting present and prospective dangers.

Because Herbert Rosinski did not live to complete his task, the book to which he dedicated his mature years is destined to remain an unfinished monument. Conscious of the insufficiency of human thought and language to grasp the deeper aspects of experience, he never ceased to strive for new and better formulations and to explore new facets of the virtually unlimited undertaking to which he had set himself. A preliminary version of the present work, completed in 1960 under the auspices of The Twentieth Century Fund, aroused wide interest in America and abroad but failed to satisfy the author's own meticulous sense of responsibility. He therefore set out to rework the entire subject, writing this time in the German language, the medium that had remained the most congenial to his intellectual processes even after a quarter-century in the English-speaking world. In his very last weeks, during the winter of 1961–62, he was much occupied with certain new philosophical insights into the nature of power that, had he lived, would undoubtedly have led to further refinements in many portions of the work.

The sense of ethical commitment that pervades Rosinski's book has been most helpful in sustaining the editorial courage required to complete it for publication. The incomplete condition of the author's manuscripts necessitated a good deal of translation, rewriting, transposition, condensation, and even elaboration, so that the final result is not so much a transcription as a restatement of the author's main ideas, sometimes in his own words but quite often in language that seemed to me to approximate more closely the form that he would ultimately have preferred. This type of editorial license has been especially necessary in the concluding chapter, which attempts to develop a coherent discussion out of the author's fragmentary but always illuminating notes and preliminary drafts. While no one operating in this fashion can pretend that every detail of his work would have the author's approval, I am reasonably confident that I have nowhere done violence to his basic intentions.

It would be quite impossible to list the innumerable individuals, living and dead, who contributed in some measure to the unique intellectual development of which this book is the product. While I have tried to see that proper acknowledgment is made in the case of those writings that have clearly influenced the discussion in a significant way, I must ask pardon in advance for any inadvertent omissions in this respect. Among the individuals who have been more directly connected with the project at one or another of its several stages, special thanks are due above all to August Heckscher, Director of The Twentieth Century Fund, for his far-seeing support of both author and editor over a lengthening period of years. Louise Field of The Twentieth Century Fund provided important assistance in clarifying the language and structure of the version that serves as the foundation for much of the present text. Elaine P. Adam rendered invaluable and generous technical aid both during the author's lifetime and subsequently. Phyllis Freeman, of the house of Frederick A. Praeger, has been a wise and sympathetic counselor in all that concerns the mysteries of publication. It should be added that neither The Twentieth

Century Fund nor the individuals mentioned are in any way answerable for the version now offered to the public, for which the undersigned assumes full responsibility.

My own relationship to the enterprise has been that of a close friend and professional colleague who was privileged to discuss it with the author on many occasions and thus found it not unnatural to confront the hazards involved in trying to bring his work to a conclusion. Apart from a sense of personal obligation, it seemed to me that such an effort might tend to mitigate in some small degree the tragedy of the author's death in the midst of an undertaking for which he himself had sacrificed so much. Throughout his life Herbert Rosinski fought unremittingly in the cause of the human spirit and against the insidious depersonalizing forces of our time. How far these intense and frequently almost singlehanded efforts may have been worth the price will depend in no small measure on the readers of this book.

RICHARD P. STEBBINS

Contents

Power and Human Destiny

I

The Meaning of Power

EACH YEAR it becomes more evident that we stand at the opening of an entirely new chapter in the story of man's development. Since the beginning of this century, our environment has been going through a fundamental transformation that involves more radical changes in the conditions of existence than mankind has ever before experienced. This transformation goes so deep, its ramifications are so intertwined, and its pace has been accelerating to such a degree that we are not merely bewildered but virtually overwhelmed by it. To grasp its meaning and extent, we must do more than just look about us. We must also look backward and forward—backward to our origins, forward as far as our gaze can penetrate the future. Only through such a general view can we hope to understand the transformation in which we are participating—and, with it, the imperative of our times.

THE UPWARD MARCH OF MANKIND

Behind us there stretches the long and painful upward course of mankind from the darkness of its beginnings into the light and clarity of our present. We do not know exactly when this strange and fascinating course began—roughly some 500,000 or 600,000

years ago, when our earliest human forebears first raised themselves in a decisive manner above their fellow animals. Closely
united, like the latter, in groups and hordes, they wandered over
the open terrain between hills, glaciers, forests, and tropical
jungles, seeking their nourishment through hunting, fishing, and
the gathering of edible plants and fruits.

For approximately 500,000 years these widely scattered human
groups remained at their original primitive level. Gradually they
acquired the basic elements of human existence—fire, tools,
language, the beginnings of religion and art. Yet fundamental as
they were, no one of these elements raised man above his first
rudimentary stage. Only around 10,000 years before our time—
presumably 8000 B.C. at the earliest—did man advance to the
second great stage of human development, that of settlement,
agriculture, and animal husbandry.

The decisive significance of this "agricultural revolution," as it
has been called, has been fully understood only in our own time
in the light of the much deeper and even more far-reaching transformation we ourselves are going through. For it was a real
revolution—a radical, comprehensive transformation of the whole
of human existence. The transition from hunting and trapping to
agriculture and animal husbandry revolutionized not merely the
economic and material basis of life but the whole of man's spiritual and intellectual orientation, toward nature and toward his
fellow men. In contrast to the fundamental discoveries which had
occurred during the hunting epoch, it was not merely a decisive
advance in this or that specialized field but an ascent from one
whole style of existence to another that was both different and
incomparably higher.

From its beginnings in the Near East and possibly in a second
independent center in Southeast Asia, the agricultural revolution
gradually spread around the earth. From all that we can infer,
such a transformation in depth must have lasted for a considerable time. Nevertheless it remained a single, once-for-all step.
Once the transition was accomplished, the different human groups

settled down on their higher plateau of existence. For another 10,000 years, more or less, agriculture and animal husbandry would still remain the basis of all further development. The basic material forms of human existence—housing, nourishment, clothing, and travel—would continue essentially on the same level, however extended and diversified. The same was true of the basic forms of spiritual and intellectual development and human coexistence—the modes of belief, of political rule, of social relationships. All of these had their roots in the world that had been given to man by nature, a world that corresponded to man's capabilities and measure, one that he was able to survey and dominate intellectually. These forms of development faithfully reflected the constancy of the basic elements of existence—the nature of man himself, men's ways of living together, the stable values of material and spiritual goods. All of these elements were basically conservative in character. The emphasis was on harmony, stability, and durability rather than on change, innovation, and progress.

Three occurrences in the course of this long period, which we have come to designate as the "agricultural era," carried matters a decisive step further. The first was the appearance of the so-called High Civilizations, which developed out of the original peasant cultures in the course of the fourth millennium B.C. Appearing first on the Nile, the Euphrates and Tigris, and the Indus (and, at least a thousand years later, on the Hwang Ho), these High Civilizations for the first time consolidated extensive tracts of territory in the basins of the great rivers and gave them a unified cultural stamp. Whether they first arose in response to the practical tasks of regulating the river waters, through the conquest of the peasant cultures by warlike pastoral tribes, or through some combination of the two, the High Civilizations constituted completely novel forms, the first large-scale and highly developed forms of political and social organization. Indicative of their strongly individualized and sharply defined character is the fact that two of these original High Civilizations, those of India and

China, maintained themselves in undiminished strength through all the fateful changes of five thousand years right down to our own time. Although the two Near Eastern civilizations of Egypt and Mesopotamia did not survive as such, they nevertheless provided the foundations on which were later to develop both our Western civilization and the world of Islam. The High Civilizations consolidated and fulfilled the spiritual and intellectual impulses that had developed with man's transition to a settled life and to agriculture. In them, the primitive fertility myths of the peasant cultures reappeared in a more highly developed and spiritualized form.

A second decisive step in mankind's development during the agricultural period was the confrontation and ultimate coming to terms with these mythological conceptions that lay at the basis of the great agricultural civilizations. This confrontation takes the form of a series of religious and philosophical advances that began during the first millennium B.C. and makes itself felt in all of the High Civilizations. This "Axis Period" is that of Confucius and Lao-tse in China, the Upanishads, Buddhism, and Jainism in India, the prophetic mission of Zoroaster in the Persian realm, the great prophets of Israel in the Near East, the breakthrough from *mythos* to *logos* in Greece. Much as they differ among themselves, each of these movements accomplished in its own fashion the break with the mythological world pictures or cosmologies of the earlier agricultural stage. In the East, in China, Japan, and India, this break remained a partial development within the framework of the existing cultures—an affair of small elites that did not affect the attitude of the broad masses. In Israel and in Greece, in contrast, the break was radical and comprehensive. It is from this point onward that the West begins to separate itself from the East.

Thus the third decisive step in man's development during the agricultural age was not carried out in equal measure by all of the High Civilizations, but was primarily the achievement of the Western branch. During the early centuries of our era the Judeo-

Christian tradition, with its compelling religious drives, was united with the unique rational force of Greece and the emotional impulses of the northern barbarian peoples. From the amalgamation of these separate elements there developed in the course of the Middle Ages a movement in the West of such overwhelming explosive force that within a few centuries it would radically disrupt the spiritual and intellectual structure which had taken form over so many thousands of years. All of the fundamental traits that had hitherto determined men's thoughts and feelings now began to be transformed into their opposites. Not the old and familiar, but the new and untried began to seem valuable and important. Man's striving was no longer directed toward accommodation to the cosmos and its laws, but toward becoming their absolute master. It was no longer a question of preserving, but rather of grasping at the uttermost possibilities and even transcending them.

This breakthrough of the forces of modern Western civilization followed two main lines of development. Externally, it led the states of Europe to a world-wide expansion through which, in the course of four centuries, they extended their power over all the rest of the world and for the first time imposed a measure of unity upon it. Internally, it led to the development of modern civilization, first in the consolidation of the modern state and state system, then, through the development of modern science and technology, to the industrial revolution—which, starting in the economic realm, soon began to subject all other areas of human existence to an increasing and ever more radical transformation. In the First World War these two processes of expansion and internal transformation united in such a way as to bring to a final conclusion the agricultural stage of human development—which had increasingly become a hollow shell, politically, socially, and spiritually—and to introduce a new, third main stage in the evolution of mankind.

The transformation in which we now find ourselves caught up resembles the agricultural revolution in the sense that it involves a radical and all-inclusive transformation of our whole existence, not only in its material foundations but equally in its political, social, spiritual, and intellectual structure. The more closely we compare the two processes, however, the more sharply the differences between them emerge.

The first of these differences has to do with the scope and dimensions of the transformation itself. Though the agricultural revolution did in fact involve a transition from a lower to a higher cultural stage, mankind still remained in its natural environment —indeed, more firmly rooted in it than before. What was fundamentally different about the industrial revolution was that it raised us to a stage that is radically new both quantitatively and qualitatively, transporting us out of the natural world of man into a new environment which transcends our natural environment in the most far-reaching manner. Our new industrial civilization no longer represents the naturally given world of man, a familiar world in which we can feel at home, a world adapted to our measure, which we can survey in all its extent. With its indissoluble tangle of relationships and its massive concentrations of men and economic forces, our civilization forms a completely new kind of world that threatens to overwhelm all our capabilities of understanding. It has already transformed us in a far deeper fashion than we realize, and it continues to make ever-increasing demands on our adaptability.

In contrast to the agricultural revolution, moreover, this new revolution is not a single step complete in itself. Instead of coming to a conclusion as the agricultural revolution did, the industrial revolution has continued to broaden itself in an unceasing process of transformation, a process that is still going forward on an increasing scale and in an ever-deeper and more accelerated manner. This constant transformation of our world has become the fundamental principle of our industrial age. Where the basic attitude of the agricultural period emphasized consolidation, permanence, and continuity, the experience of constant transformation in our industrial era has led to an equally definite emphasis on the conscious desire for innovation—and not merely on innovation in general, as has been true throughout the period, but quite specifically on planned and continuous innovation. It is not merely that the plenitude of new insights and methods which has been constantly flooding in upon us has put us in a position to substitute for the traditional, inherited, and purely fortuitous forms of existence an increasingly planned analysis and systematic reordering of our life. These systematic reconstitutions of our existence and our world are no longer seen as one-time, definitive transformations but simply as steps in a continuous process of further development in which each individual stage is destined to be surpassed and transcended in its turn.

Nature and Man

The sense of freedom to shape his own destiny that has thus become the hallmark of contemporary man amounts to a well-nigh total reversal of the conditions prevailing at man's origin. For the development of man begins not in a state of freedom but in a state of absolute bondage and total subjection to natural laws and forces.

This bondage has three fundamental aspects. In the widest sense, it is a bondage to physical nature: to climate, to the rhythms of nature, to the relative abundance or scarcity of nourishment, clothing, shelter.

Second is the bondage to man's human environment, to his immediate family and to the wider community of which it forms a part. This bondage to his own kind is all the more decisive for man's outlook because his individual period of maturation lasts for almost a third of his normal life span. Throughout this long period he is almost helplessly exposed to the operation of his environment, even though he is quite unconscious of the fact and wholly incapable of withdrawing from or defending himself against these environmental influences.

The third and most intimate form of bondage is man's bondage to himself and to his own animal existence as a manifestation of nature. Not only is he bound to an animal body, with its animal functions of development, reproduction, and senescence; he is even more intimately bound to an animal soul, one whose drives and impulses are not basically different from those of his fellow animals but are only distinguished from them by the degree of his development. However deeply man explores this soul of his, within its innermost recesses he still finds himself under the spell and in the bondage of nature. Only on the innermost frontier of his animal soul does he finally come up against the one thing in him which no longer lies within the bondage of nature—his Self.

Thus the real development of man could only begin with a radical break, a rupture with this absolute bondage to nature; and such a break could begin only from this innermost point in his soul. The only way in which he could become aware of his unique quality as man, of his specific humanness, was by radically differentiating himself from all of nature and setting himself up against her in virtue of this very differentness. Only through such a break in his innermost root could man become aware of himself in those things that differentiate him from all his fellow animals —in other words, in his nonanimal self—and thus in a fundamental sense raise himself above them all. The way in which man established himself in his unique humanness, in other words, was not through the fulfillment of his natural endowment but rather through his rupture with it.

This radical break was at first only an implicit, not an explicit one. As was to happen so often in man's later activities, the action in this most fundamental of all his steps ran far, far ahead of his consciousness of it. For it was only on the basis of this concrete action establishing him as Man that his self-consciousness as Man could little by little begin to develop. Consciousness of Self had to be preceded by the formation of the Self. Our earliest ancestors carried out this radical step without in any way willing it or even realizing what had happened. Indeed, it is only today that the full sense and inner necessity of this differentiation, as it emerges from the opposition of man's animal origin on one side and his rejection of it on the other, meets us in a compellingly clear-cut fashion.

This deeper insight into man's origin through his unique break with the bondage of nature enables us to comprehend his special character more clearly. More than at any earlier time, we are becoming aware that what constitutes man's nature is not any one of the special characteristics by which men in the course of their development have sought to define themselves—not reason, not the capacity for political coexistence, not work, and also not technique—but simply and solely the fact of this radical break with nature. Man is the form of life whose unique position derives specifically from his capacity for this unique break—from his capacity to establish himself as a Self, and, on the basis of this Self, to achieve detachment from himself, to take a position toward himself, and in this way to raise himself essentially above himself. And, of course, to do so not just once, in his origin, but continuously. Man thus acquires the character not of any once-and-for-all, qualitatively fixed being, but rather of a process of becoming, of humanization—of a historical process which, after being set in motion by the original break with nature and carried forward by the impulses deriving from this break, leads into a continuity of self-transformation, self-conquest, and self-surpassing. Man thus appears not as nature, but as history.

Yet the more clearly we become aware of this unique human capability, the more mysterious it becomes. Modern anthropology has catalogued an infinitude of the most varied biological traits that help to explain how man could arrive at his unique break with nature: his erect posture, the frontal development of his head, especially the eyes, the expansion of his field of activity through the freedom of his movements, and so forth. But these are merely favorable factors that tell us *how* man's radical break with nature could come about. They do not clearly explain *why* it did occur. The inner impulse that drove man to this act evades any such causal explanation and remains simply incomprehensible.

This inscrutability is equally characteristic of man's entire further development. Man does not raise himself above the bondage of nature in this radical fashion simply in order to pursue his further development according to rationally ascertainable mechanical or dialectical laws. His whole further development seems permeated by these same inexplicable impulses, not only in each individual human existence but, above all, in the decisive steps in the development of mankind as a whole. Precisely in these decisive steps—in the transition to settlement, in the development of the High Civilizations, in the shedding of the bondage of mythology, in the breakthrough to the modern era—the more deeply we try to see into their causes, the more strongly we feel that all of the developmental tendencies that point toward them are wholly insufficient to explain them satisfactorily.

The nature of man's origin determines also the character of his further evolution. Originating in the bondage of nature, he can free himself only by wresting from nature one by one the individual bonds that confine him. It is in thus shaking off one bond after another that man gradually wins from nature his recognition of himself, his ability to form his human environment, his domination over physical nature. By gaining this measure of independence, he wins for himself a realm which he can survey, form, and rule—a realm that constitutes his world.

At the same time, this world of his still remains a mere fragment, a piece cut out from surrounding nature. However far he may advance his frontiers at nature's expense, it still remains only a limited realm within the unlimited and unsurveyable extent of nature itself. It remains a clearing in a boundless wilderness through which he can never force his way into the open. All his understanding, all his action, however greatly it may surpass his former limits, still brings him only to new limits. The process of progressive self-liberation from the bondage of nature thus remains always a limited process and, in light of the unlimited character of nature itself, must necessarily remain an unending process.

The Anatomy of Power

As he thus develops himself and little by little conquers a living space from surrounding nature, man unavoidably involves himself in the dialectic of power. For it is by bringing power into being that man develops. The only way in which he could free himself from the bondage of nature was by substituting for the "organic" living sphere of nature the "artificial" living sphere of his self-chosen, self-developed way of life, or culture. To do this he needed to develop the power to create for himself this new world of culture—new foods, tools, shelter, fire, rites, customs, traditions, societies. Mankind's unceasing quest for freedom was absolutely dependent upon the development of more and more power, higher and higher levels of power. Man's quest for freedom and his quest for power have been but the two faces of a single coin.

Man's progress in the development of power has been a process of long duration and of an infinite complexity, which to this day has tended to obscure the deep and difficult issues it involves. To begin to understand them, we must divorce ourselves so far as possible from current intellectual conventions and try to look at power not in terms of the abstract or fragmentary conceptions that figure so widely in contemporary discussion, but rather as the basic condition of our entire existence.

Any reasonable discussion of the problem of power as it has grown and developed through the centuries must begin by recognizing that the term "power" needs to be applied in an unusually comprehensive sense before we can hope to understand the reality behind the word. We shall get nowhere by thinking of power as an element that is encountered in political or military affairs but is absent, or can be excluded, from the other relations of life. Nor is it fruitful to invoke the psychological concept of a primal "will to power" which we can either encourage or discourage and which, conceivably, we might be able to educate away entirely. Far from limiting our conception of power in any of these ways, we need to extend it as broadly as possible. For power, in the sense in which the term will be used throughout this book, is the reverse of a limited or partial concept. Power is nothing less than an objective quality of all reality, a quality inherent in all that exists by virtue of the mere fact that it does exist. Power is an inescapable aspect of reality itself.

Strange though it may appear to our contemporary minds, this universal view of power, this perception of the infinite multitude of existing things as so many manifestations of power, was a matter of course to all the earlier civilizations. Their different world views were simply different ways of recognizing and interpreting a fundamental sense of the world as an order, or cosmos, of many different powers. Such a sense of the universality of power is typified, though in quite different ways, by the two traditions that were to become the main roots of our Western civilization, the Biblical and the Graeco-Roman. Nowhere is the connection between being, or reality, and power more strikingly exemplified than in the Biblical interpretation of the sacred name of God as "THE I AM." The Graeco-Roman civilization, in its own quite different fashion, was equally emphatic in its recognition of this relationship, of the universal character of power amid its multiple manifestations.

It was only with the radical change that came over Western civilization at the beginning of the modern era that this earlier view of power began to be discarded. In a sense, the simplification and limitation of the concept of power that then set in was a necessary condition of further progress. Only by stripping the natural world of those mythical powers attributed to it by Scholastic philosophy (following Aristotle) could a path be cleared for a more realistic analysis of the actual physical structure of the universe. Only by stripping the political world of the mythico-religious significance with which the Middle Ages had invested it could the way be cleared for a sober analysis of the realities of political power, such as we find in Machiavelli. In no other way, finally, could the Western mind be freed for what may have been the most significant of all the developments of modern Western civilization, the idea of a "private sphere" in which the individual discovered for the first time a fully autonomous field of action.

But if this process of "disenchantment" in relation to the idea of power was indispensable in order that Western man might go forward to his subsequent marvelous achievements, it also led to new misconceptions that we are only now beginning to recognize and overcome. In eliminating from our view of the world the confusing, mythical forms in which the varied manifestations of power had hitherto been conceived, we quite unwarrantably restricted our notion of power and began to conceive it as something confined essentially to the political and military fields. In his discovery of the "private sphere," which by definition lay wholly outside the political and military areas, Western man entirely overlooked the possibility that purely private activities would also develop in such massive dimensions that they, too, would become a source of power that would cry out for responsible recognition and control. Even the notion of energy in the natural processes was treated as something altogether different from, and unrelated to, political and military power.

The result has been the strangely divided attitude toward power that has characterized modern Western civilization throughout its course. Power of every conceivable kind has been developing on a scale that staggers the imagination; yet we have remained most reluctant to draw the inevitable conclusions. In none of the major theories of society and politics of the last two centuries have the problems posed by this tremendous buildup of energies in industrial mass societies been adequately recognized. They have no place in the ideology of Western democracy, which is still thinking mainly in the terms of the eighteenth-century Enlightenment and the Manchester School. They were only very partially recognized by Hegel, because he thought mainly in the political terms of the French Revolution. Nor were they recognized by Marx, who similarly turned away from the reality of power in order to dream of a power-free, world-wide "society of free men." Whatever our intellectual heritage, all of us have preferred in greater or less degree to ignore the realities of power and the problems of recognition and control with which it confronts us. Instead, we have indulged in daydreams of an increasingly power-free

world that would be freed from all concern with this most decisive and challenging aspect of our existence.

It is true that the events of our own time have served in a
measure to free us from these illusions and bring us closer to the
realities. The two World Wars and, above all, the unprecedented
arms race since 1950 have made the idea of a separation of our
activities into watertight civilian and military compartments less
and less tenable. We have at least begun to perceive the way in
which virtually all forms of civilian activity—agriculture and industry, transportation, medicine, education, even the theater,
ballet, chess, and sports—have been transformed into instruments
of an ever-widening politico-military power struggle. It is no
longer so easy to overlook the fact that such cultural, social, economic, or psychological activities, pursued on a sufficiently large
mass scale, themselves become a source of power that is politically
significant, is subject to political manipulation, and demands to
be understood and controlled. In this limited sense, at least, we
are beginning to return to the fundamental fact about power that
was instinctively realized by the older civilizations: namely, that
so far from being confined to the political and military sphere or
to the "public" aspect of man's activities, power is in the most
literal sense all-embracing. We are beginning to recognize, no
longer in naïve mythical images but in quite sober terms, that
everything that is, every bit of reality, is in its own way a part of
power, and that at our present level of development these frag-
ments tend to pile up into mass effects of hitherto unknown
potency.

But while these fundamental facts about the nature of power
have undoubtedly begun to be felt here and there, their recognition has thus far been all too fragmentary and incomplete. To a
considerable extent our perceptions have been limited to the area
of the Cold War, where the universal nature of power and the
variety of its forms have been most conspicuous. So far, we have
not even begun to face the problem in terms of our civilization as
a whole, or to correlate and analyze the different manifestations

of power in systematic fashion. Before we can even begin to think of coping with the tremendous increase of power that distinguishes our age, we must make a more coherent attempt to understand what power actually is, how it develops, and the kind of effects that it produces. In doing so we shall be availing ourselves of—but will not be limited by—the important insights achieved by Hegel and Marx in the early years of the industrial revolution. Both of these towering thinkers were much concerned with the problem of power, although their specific contributions to its understanding can be better appreciated when we come to examine the special conditions in which they confronted its still primitive manifestations during the first half of the nineteenth century.

POWER AND COUNTERPOWER

In seeking an understanding of power more adequate to our contemporary situation, our first task is to realize that the power which pervades our world is not an undifferentiated whole but exists in two main forms that correspond to different aspects of reality itself. This distinction reflects the essentially dynamic character of the reality of which power is one of the manifestations. As Hegel emphasized 150 years ago, reality is something more than mere "being" or "given fact." Nothing ever merely *is*. Whatever exists—inanimate matter, plants, animals, man and his works—exists as the result of a process of development or "realization."

This idea, which was as familiar to the Greeks as it was to later philosophy, is much easier for us to grasp today in view of the discoveries of the past 100 years. One by one, we have discovered the processes by which the different forms of existence have come or are coming to be "realized." Nuclear physics has shown us that the atom, that seemingly most solid of all existing things, has itself come into being by virtue of the tendency of energy to realize itself as "matter"—that is, as a core surrounded by electrons. Application of nuclear physics has indicated that the entire universe, as far as our observations reach, is built up and determined by the same processes. In the same way, chemistry has shown us the manner in which atoms combine into molecules; biology has taught us how molecules have been built up into organic matter, and how organic matter has tended to produce life. Evolution presents a theory of how life has developed, from the simplest forms through a long series of stages to man himself. Psychoanalysis has given us new insights into how our personalities, too, result from a largely unself-conscious process of realization. Finally, our study of history increasingly shows how the whole development of mankind is nothing but a vast process of realization—a process of which we now stand at a culminating point, looking backward upon all that has led up to us and forward to the incredibly difficult task of ensuring that it will be enabled to continue.

In the perspective thus opened up, the whole universe appears as a gigantic process of realization, a gushing forth of a constant stream of energies of every kind—electrical charges, biological urges, animal instincts, psychological impulses, the conscious wills and designs of men—which crystallize into manifold forms of reality. This flood of energies produces inanimate matter, plants and animals, men and the works of their thoughts and hands, their languages, institutions, customs and usages.

Yet to think of the evolution of the universe as simply a process in which different energies are "realized" into innumerable forms of reality is to make it appear too natural, too obvious, and too easy. The universe would then appear simply as the natural and inevitable result of the streams of energies that pulse through its veins. In emphasizing the general "forward" tendency of this universal process, we tend to eliminate, or at least to minimize, all opposing tendencies. Actually, the processes of realization are not simply the result of the free flow of energies and their crystallization, because these forces are by no means unimpeded but invariably have to struggle against obstacles that may halt them or give them an altogether new direction. Thus what *is* is not simply the result of an effortless process of realization, but of an interplay of conflicting forces. The transformation of energy into reality takes place by way of a rigorous process of selection. The different energies—the electric impulses in the nuclear world, the different germs, the thoughts and designs of men—tend to conflict with or destroy one another. There are always far more of these forces than can find realization, either simultaneously or successively. Of these innumerable energies, relatively few will actually succeed in struggling through into reality. Fewer still will succeed in running the whole course of their natural existence.

Thus everything that becomes reality goes through a continual struggle for realization. In nature, it is a struggle for mere existence and survival. Man, too, must fight for survival, but he is also involved in a nobler kind of struggle—one for self-realization. Man is above all a creator, and must struggle to bring into being those things upon which he has set his heart and for which he is ready to shed his heart's blood. It is this passionate character of the struggle that gives those few energies that actually win through their unique significance as bits of reality. Each bit of reality represents a force that has come to fulfillment, something that has shown itself to be truly power by having asserted its capability of being. For the purposes of our analysis, this may most appropriately be described as active or "subjective" power.

But the unique character of reality as the realization of subjective powers of every kind is not its only aspect, though it is the one on which the study of power has hitherto been almost exclusively concentrated. Reality—and power—have another side, which even those who have been most aware have not brought out clearly or systematically. Reality at any given moment is not simply the end product of a process of realization; it is also an established fact that represents the starting point of a further process of development. As with reality, so it is with power. In addition to the "subjective" power manifested in the process of becoming, there is also the "objective" power inherent in the established fact itself. This is the power that, having come into being as the end product of a successful process of realization, stands as realized, established, objectified power, ready to exert its own influence in the endless chain of being. It is reality in its other character as an objective force.

In terms of our everyday language, any subjective power that has become objectified as reality has thereby become an established fact. As such, it has acquired a number of qualities that together constitute its "objective" power. In the first place, it does not simply exist. It is emphatically *there* as part of the world of established facts. As a particular and unique bit of reality, it has acquired a definite position, shape, and nature. Its existence in this particular position, shape, and nature contributes its specific part to the sum total of all realities. If it were different in any of these respects, the world of real things would to that extent be different from what it is.

Second, as a unique part of reality, our "established fact" exercises an influence upon other real things. Reality is characterized by objective power precisely because each bit of it has the capacity of acting upon other bits of reality and influencing them in its turn. Conversely, this reality itself is subject to being acted upon and influenced by other established realities.

Third, as an established fact, each bit of reality possesses a greater or lesser measure of durability. It does not possess the eternal durability that Aristotle erroneously attributed to the stars, but only a widely variable degree of limited durability. But as long as it is not destroyed by a process of nuclear fission, organic decay, or biological death, it holds its position and generally is able to offer a very considerable degree of resistance to any effort to dislodge it.

To illustrate these abstract statements by a concrete example, a mountain range is an established fact. It has its unique position, its peculiar geological stratification, state of erosion, height, and appearance, and its sphere of influence. It influences the weather, determines the course of rivers, and provides refuge and protection for wild life and for human beings. It may influence the economic and cultural development of a people by the food it provides, the minerals in its veins, the water power of its streams. Finally, it has its particular degree of durability, depending primarily on whether it happens to be composed of harder or softer materials. In the same fashion, plants and animals, human institutions and usages, political regimes, even languages and civilizations, also constitute "established facts" and exercise a comparable type of objective power.

These two aspects of reality, and the power that goes with them, do not simply exist back to back like the two faces of a coin. In man's struggle to develop his power, to free himself from the bondage of his environment and organize his world according to his own desires, they confront each other and become engaged in an interplay of reactions. Inevitably, the things that man creates become objectified as established facts which thereupon begin to exercise a power of their own. Ordinarily, this is a wholly unintended process. In the overwhelming majority of cases, man simply creates the things he needs and desires without giving any thought to the objective power they are bound to exercise. How often does a new invention, a new book lead to consequences unforeseen by its author? Even if he is aware of this longer-range aspect of his activities, he may not wish to produce the particular result in question. Nevertheless, all man's actions necessarily create objective power, whether or not he recognizes or desires it.

The objective power that is thus brought into being is, moreover, a highly ambiguous quantity, one whose operation may be either beneficial or harmful. To take an obvious example, the development of medicine to a point where it could deal effectively with infectious diseases also let loose upon the world a body of knowledge that can be abused and perverted for use in bacteriological warfare. Conversely, the development of the atomic bomb as an instrument of destruction also opened an avenue to the use of atomic energy for peaceful purposes. These examples suffice to suggest that all power, all capacity to exercise effort and to influence the course of events, is by nature ambiguous, "open," and neutral or indeterminate in its implications. Were it not equally potent for good and for evil, it would not be power at all.

This ambiguity is all the greater because the objective power that man brings into being inevitably challenges his own ability to control it. Man's actions invariably produce wider consequences than he himself intends. So long as he remains engaged in the process of creation, the objective power of his acts remains under his control. But once his creation has become realized and begins to exercise power in its own right, it becomes independent of his original intention and also of his endeavors to maintain control over it. He cannot prevent this development, any more than he can protect anything he has created from being abused and perverted by others.

But we have yet to name the most formidable characteristic of the objective power inherent in man's own works. In its ultimate consequences, the buildup of objective power tends to turn *against man himself*. By each of his actions man establishes independent, obstinate, obdurate facts that are by no means easy to undo again, even if experience proves them to be highly inconvenient and undesirable. To repeal a law, abolish an institution, or eliminate a practice that is no longer in the general interest invariably requires an effort, often a considerable one. Not only does this new effort call for energy that may be more profitably applied elsewhere; in the normal course of events, it tends to require more energy than did the original establishment of the fact in question. Except in extreme cases, therefore, the natural tendency is to let established facts persist even when they are recognized to be harmful.

Thus we are confronted by three of the fundamental and inescapable conditions of man's struggle for self-liberation: first, the things he creates almost immediately begin to escape from his control and to assume an independent existence of their own; second, they invariably lead to consequences that were neither foreseen nor intended; and third, they may turn out to be highly inconvenient and to require great efforts if they are to be undone. By every fact that man establishes, he thus tends to limit his own freedom of action. Creation tends to result not in self-liberation but in self-limitation. Power turns into something which may appropriately be called "counterpower."

The paradox of this situation lies in the very nature of man's struggle for power. The central purpose of that struggle is precisely to free himself from the multiple bonds of nature amid which he first awakened to the consciousness of himself and of his special human destiny. Yet in the very act of freeing himself from these primeval bonds, man sets up new forces whose effect is to threaten his new-found freedom from a totally new angle. The very qualities that enabled him to raise himself so radically above his fellow animals carry within them the threat of a new and even more fateful bondage.

For man, unlike his animal predecessors, was not tied down by instinct or physical equipment to any stereotyped form of life or to any closely limited environment. His innate restlessness enabled him to rise far above such limitations. He could settle down anywhere and try his hand at anything. Above all, he developed the capacity for constant change, the ability to tear out his roots and try to improve his lot by starting afresh. Thus he could utilize the power of his gradually awakening intelligence and skills to gain greater freedom by creating tools and other artifacts, shelter and well-being in the form of houses, villages, cities; of customs, institutions, societies, civilizations.

Yet in thus freeing himself from nature by building up an artificial world of his own creation, man was also forging for himself new fetters in place of those he had cast off. For tools and shelter, institutions and societies are so many established facts. In creating them through the exercise of his subjective power, man could not prevent the objective power inherent in his own works from becoming consolidated into an objective world with a consistency of its own. In due course he finds himself enmeshed in a world whose structure and relationships he no longer controls or even understands, a world that has suddenly turned into an alien power opposed to him—a world of counterpower.

The inherent limitation imposed on man by the development of objective power becomes more and more accentuated as his separate and varied works become intertwined and consolidated in those vast organizations of all aspects of human existence that we call civilizations. Like the huge coral reefs of the Pacific, built up by the activities of millions and millions of polyps into gigantic labyrinthine structures, our civilizations are the product of the actions of millions of people over thousands of years. In the long process of building up these complex cultural structures, men are apt to lose all understanding of the original impulses that went into their development, and to find themselves limited by their own creations in the most drastic fashion without even realizing that they are so limited or how they have come to be so. Thus it seems at times as if man's age-old struggle for freedom was destined to become finally a mere pilgrimage from one bondage to another, from the "organic" bondage of nature to the "mechanical" bondage of culture.

THE PROBLEM OF CONTROL

It is at this crucial point that we come face to face with the essential problem inherent in man's development of power. Man *must* strive for power. He has no alternative. His quest for power is his "nature." It is this that has raised him above all other animals, and it is the presupposition of his advance in freedom. Having pursued this quest so far, he cannot possibly stop the process. Yet, as the artificial world of his creation becomes more and more saturated with power of every kind, it also becomes more and more complex and more and more difficult to understand and control. Thus our quest for freedom threatens to end in a radical self-contradiction, if not in absolute self-destruction.

There is only one way out of this dilemma. Although we cannot stop the process whereby objective power is being built up, we can, perhaps, prevent it from escaping our understanding and control and thus consolidating itself irrevocably into counterpower. We cannot continue to increase power blindly and still hope to escape, somehow, the inevitable consequences of our own blindness. We must come to recognize, first, that every action constitutes in smaller or larger measure the creation of power; and, second, that all creation of power must henceforth become a two-sided process. It must be a process in which the responsible recognition and control of power goes hand in hand with its creation. It must be a process in which we shall be continually on guard to prevent the constant buildup of objective power from getting out of hand, accumulating, and turning into counterpower.

The fundamental problem raised by man's quest for power is as old as man himself. In former ages, however, it was not so acute. It can be argued that at the generally low level of power prevailing in former civilizations, its tendency to turn into counterpower actually added to the stability of the relatively weak cultural patterns characteristic of those times. Traditions and customs, even though they tended to change from live impulses into what Hegel called "external rules and mechanical usages," helped to consolidate and stabilize the cultural framework. When this process went too far, new impulses periodically overthrew the obsolete structure. But at the level of power then prevailing, even these convulsions seldom reached catastrophic dimensions.

The problem has become radically different with the tremendous forces that Western civilization has set in motion over the past five hundred years. What we are confronted with today is no longer simply the danger that man in his blind development of power will find himself increasingly fettered in a world he no longer understands or controls—and in which, moreover, he is generally not even aware of the fact. What we are concerned with today is more than merely our freedom—our very survival is at stake. By our continued failure to recognize the effort needed to maintain effective control over the results of our activities, we are

beginning to imperil not only our freedom but our physical existence. Day by day, we continue to fill our world with such overwhelming, interacting forces of every kind that unless we can
manage to reassert our control, they will become so entangled and
concentrated as to threaten quite literally to crush us. Far from
being limited to the possibility of an exchange of thermonuclear
weapons, the only aspect of the problem that has thus far been
given due attention, this threat pervades our entire situation.

The danger is all the greater because the ever-increasing dynamism of our industrial mass societies ordinarily tends to conceal
itself under a surface of streamlined smoothness. Our vast organizations, public and private, our more and more complex mass
processes in industry, transportation, communications, appear like
so many rushing streams on which the individual is effortlessly
borne along. The exhilarating sense of flow tends to disguise the
surging power behind and within it.

This smoothness, however, is deceptive. With the increasing
concentration of each individual upon his own immediate desires
and purposes, we fail to recognize the objective forces that these
processes create. Small in the individual case, this objective power
is multiplied by the concurrent actions of millions of people.
Normally these vast, unrecognized, and uncontrolled masses of
power continue to float, so to speak, upon different streams. But
at moments of crisis, such as we have witnessed in the two World
Wars and in the Great Depression, they suddenly assert themselves. It is as if the normally submerged masses of power suddenly congealed into huge ice floes, crashing into each other and
crushing everything that comes between them.

Thus we can see today what both nineteenth-century liberalism
and Marxism quite failed to see—that the power we are continually creating cannot possibly be separated from our activities or
eliminated from our existence, either by slow evolution or by a
single revolutionary stroke. On the contrary, power is the inevitable by-product of all our manifold activities, and continues
to increase with their ever-increasing growth. The problem of

power is inherent in the very development of civilization, above all in our contemporary industrial civilization. It can be dealt with only in a continuous series of solutions for a continuous series of new situations. Every generation will have to face it afresh, and to find new solutions to the problem of its control.

It was Hegel who defined world history in terms of a "progress in the consciousness of freedom." But if this bold assertion is to be proved true, men will have to recognize that every advance in freedom is necessarily based upon an advance in power. They will have to recognize as well that the problem of power is complex, that it has not only its subjective side in the realization of their desires and purposes, but its bewildering and massive objective side that threatens to become a menace of untold proportions. We will have to realize that our advance in freedom can continue only if this inescapable element of objective power is not glossed over but recognized and controlled. It can be an advance in freedom only if we simultaneously advance in understanding and responsibility.

2

Power in Agricultural Civilizations

To our generation, Hegel's conception of world history as the self-realization of the spirit of freedom is bound to seem excessively abstract and one-sided, even where it is not directly in conflict with the facts of our experience. Much more congenial to the outlook of our own age is an alternative conception in which the history of mankind appears as a vast process of convergence, leading from the scattered origins of the various primeval hordes toward an ultimate unity transcending the manifold diversities of peoples and civilizations. But while this convergence toward the awakening sense of a common human consciousness and destiny can reasonably be said to represent the outline of mankind's advance through history, the underlying force that has animated this tremendous process has unmistakably been the development of man to power—a development that extends in an unbroken line from the almost complete helplessness of his original state to the independent position and abundance of powers of every conceivable kind that characterize our own age. The formidable problems created by the growth of power in our industrial society stand out all the more clearly when contrasted with the slow and gradual development of power over periods of hundreds of thousands of years amid the relatively static conditions of pre-industrial times. A review of this experience will also help to expose the roots of inconsistency in our own attitudes toward power and its various manifestations.

From Hunting to Agriculture

The history of man's involvement with power is the history of two interacting factors, man and the world around him. As with the individual, so with man as a species, the development of consciousness—and therewith of power and freedom—starts not from the self but from the world. Man's development of his consciousness and mind begins with the gradual recognition of the different elements surrounding him—natural phenomena, animals, other men—and their interweaving into a more and more integrated whole. Indeed, man's outlook has retained this essentially objective character throughout almost the entire course of his development. His advance was oriented upon the world, the cosmos, the universe of which he felt himself to be a part—and, moreover, by no means the most significant part. In the civilizations of the East, this objective orientation toward the universe has remained unbroken to this day. Even in Western civilization, it survived until the period of the Renaissance.

Thus man's gradual advance in power and freedom and independence in relation to the world around him appeared in his own eyes as simply an increasing *recognition* of the world and its powers. It was through this recognition of the powers of the world that man himself grew in consciousness and power. Hence it was but natural that men should document the growth of their consciousness and power in the form of a succession of views or pictures of the world with which they were gradually familiarizing themselves.

These world pictures in which men sought to clarify their ideas about the world and their position in it also served an eminently practical purpose. They were the intellectual instruments by which men strove increasingly to integrate their own endeavors with those of their fellow men. For the narrow limits imposed upon the individual could be transcended only by collective effort, by integrating and uniting the efforts of larger and larger groups in ever-widening circles. This development of a common way of life, supported by common endeavors, was first made possible by the invention of language. In turn, the use of language opened the way to the coordinated development of wider, loftier, and more enduring perspectives about the world. It was through this process that men were able to integrate themselves from groups into villages, from villages into territories, from territories into kingdoms and empires, and finally from localized societies into civilizations.

Unfortunately, we know far too little about the earliest and most protracted stage in man's development of power, the roving and hunting period that constitutes the basis of his whole subsequent experience. The entire period from man's earliest origins down to the commencement of settlement and agriculture, sometime after 8000 B.C., is covered with a dark veil. We know that it was in this period that such vital advances as the discovery of language, fire, and tools were made. Yet the long-continued absence of any clearly defined structural order, in tools, housing, or burial, suggests the immense difficulties that primitive man must have experienced in gradually freeing himself from his original immersion in his environment and achieving some measure of detachment and overview in relation to the impressions that crowded in upon him. The distinction between the living and the inanimate, the confrontation with the perceptible qualities of objects, the experience of natural forces and their organization into a coherent world picture obviously required a tremendous spiritual and intellectual effort. For primitive man, the world seems to have been little more than an array of widely different "beings," all animate, all bearing mysterious and ambiguous "powers," and all requiring to be approached with caution. We possess scarcely any traces of any deeper, numinous feeling that goes beyond the visible world. Art, at this original stage, is entirely lacking.

All this changes markedly with the transition to the Upper Paleolithic period, around 80,000 B.C. We now encounter a new race, the direct ancestors of our humanity of today. The tempo and variety of the cultural patrimony suddenly begins to increase by leaps and bounds. Tools become more refined and specialized. Magical conceptions associated with the hunt give birth to a first great period of artistic creation that is characterized by a marvelous skill and assurance.

Still more millennia run their slow course before the first beginnings of the agricultural revolution, somewhere around 8000 B.C. The transition from hunting to settlement and agriculture meant a tremendous forward step in man's gradual liberation from the bondage of nature; yet at the same time it subjected him all the more deeply, though in a quite novel fashion, to the bondage of these same natural forces. By freeing him from his dependence on sources of nourishment that were independent of his will and thus perennially uncertain, the agricultural revolution gave man a secure basis of existence such as he had never before enjoyed. Population density increased with extreme rapidity, according to some estimates by as much as a hundredfold. At the same time, however, this new and more assured manner of life bound man all the more closely to the forces of nature which governed it: the weather, the sun, the rain and the wind, the fertility of the earth, and the growth cycle of all living things.

The transition from hunting and fishing to the cultivation of plants and animals involved man for the first time in an intensive reciprocal relationship to these other forms of life. To live by what they provided, it was not enough simply to harvest their fruits. Man had also to lend his own efforts to assist their production. Thus he was compelled to immerse himself more and more

deeply in their conditions of life, their needs and habits, to penetrate the secrets of nature and try to adapt himself to them. In
this way man's whole relationship to nature came to be basically
transformed. If hitherto she had always appeared to him as a
fundamentally ambiguous and capricious power, it was now with
her good will that he became increasingly familiar. Nature became the great protective power, Mother Nature, in whose powerful and mysterious arms he could feel protected. Man confidently
believed in nature's spiritual and material security; she seemed an
all-comprehensive and living unity in which he, too, had his ap-
pointed place, a secure existence and beyond it the comforting
hope of a rebirth.

The growth of this first organic world picture of nature as a
unified life pattern has been traced in the writings of Adolf E.
Jensen (*Das religiöse Weltbild einer frühen Kultur*, 1948) through
the study of a widely dispersed group of ancient peoples extending from the Mediterranean basin to Southeast Asia, Mexico, and
Peru. The mysterious life of the plant world, with its annual
cycle of budding, ripening, harvesting, consumption, and renewal,
comes to be associated with the parallel cycle of animal and
human life with its generation, birth, growth, and death. From
this it is extended into a universal world picture embracing the
existence of all living things. The budding of plants is equated
with generation, their harvesting and consumption with death, or,
more exactly, with violent killing. Generation, growth, and fruit-
fulness on one side, dying and killing on the other, are intimately
associated in a unique kind of interdependence. The world seems
permeated in every direction by mysterious vital forces that were
originally called into life by the sacrifice of the chief godhead.
The most varied ritualistic ceremonies are employed to bring
about their renewal, all of them reflecting the belief in a mysterious connection between forcible bloodletting and the renewal of
vital force. Originating in the oldest period of the agricultural
civilization, this world picture survived deep into historical times
in such phenomena as the Eleusinian mysteries, continuing in its
more spiritualized survivals even into our own time.

These two factors, the fundamentally altered basis of existence and the organic world picture of nature as a unified life pattern, stamped the man of the agricultural stage in all his traits, in his feeling for life, his way of life, the tempo of his existence. He himself assimilated something plantlike into his feeling for life. In contrast to the hunter's alertness that speaks to us so unmistakably from the cave paintings of the Upper Paleolithic period, the life of the agricultural cultivator was characterized by stolidity, heaviness, and concentrated strength. His life's tempo was leisurely, his development slow and uniform.

Thus for nearly 10,000 years, up to the beginning of our own era, the basic elements of his way of life remained substantially unchanged. Societies, small or large, lived from agriculture or, more rarely, the keeping of herds. The resources, the basic grains, domestic animals, textiles, raw materials, remained remarkably uniform. Additions were made from time to time through new discoveries or through exchanges with other areas. But even such revolutionary innovations as the transition from stone to metal, the bridling of the horse, and the invention of the ship remained within this same general pattern of life. In the perspective of the development of mankind, the agricultural period thus stands out as the great period of consolidation.

THE HIGH CIVILIZATIONS

The gradual increase in power that occurred within the framework of this essentially agricultural mode of life arose not so much from any radical change in the material basis as from men's efforts to organize their existence on a larger scale and raise it to higher cultural levels. Somewhere around the transition from the fourth to the third millennium B.C. there began in four separate areas—Egypt, Mesopotamia, India, and China—the first great attempts to concentrate political power on a large scale, to amass wealth of every kind, to refine and embellish life in every way. Rather abruptly, these efforts led to the attainment of a much higher level of culture in what we call the High Civilizations, those powerful spiritual communities that were to bind together and impress their stamp upon millions of human beings over periods of thousands of years' duration.

The formation of the High Civilizations is one of those decisive events in the development of mankind that defy any causal explanation. It may be that tremendous masses of passive spiritual energy which had accumulated in the primitive peasant cultures were suddenly activated by some external impulse. Although we do not know whether or not this was the case, we may nevertheless be able to identify the external impulse in question. The far-reaching climatic changes that followed the last glacial period and gradually dried out the great belt of steppe and desert land extending across the old world encouraged a movement of population from the high plateaus into the valleys of the Nile, the Tigris and Euphrates, the Indus, and later the Hwang Ho. While the annual flooding of the swampy, alluvial lands of these deep-lying river valleys presented extraordinary obstacles to settlement, they also held extraordinary potentialities in view of the unique fertility of the soil and the assured water supply. The conquest of these obstacles and the exploitation of the accompanying potentialities represented a new and decisive forward step in man's struggle with nature.

In each of the four centers of the original High Civilizations, the first step was to coordinate the sprawling masses of isolated villages into larger units such as districts, territories, and kingdoms. The practical impulse in this direction, which arose from the need for flood control, became intertwined with such concurrent factors as the ambitions of territorial chieftains, priesthoods, or even merchant aristocracies. Whatever the motives, the coordination of these large territories inevitably required both an administrative apparatus and a military organization in the form of a militia or of picked standing forces. Writing had also to be developed, both as a means of communication over vast distances and to keep records of the more complex organization of affairs. Political integration in turn made possible a rise in production that far transcended the former village level. This surplus of production led to the development of cities—capitals or district headquarters—which became centers both of handicraft and of a remarkably far-reaching trade. Above all, the cities became the seats of the different gods which had meanwhile been emerging from the primitive fertility cults of the earliest agricultural peoples.

Like the peasant mythological cultures that preceded them, the High Civilizations were the expression of a basically religious world feeling, one that unfolded in and left its distinguishing mark on all their varied achievements in state and society, law and custom, art and science. How strongly the original religious impulse continued to operate is suggested by the fact that of the four High Civilizations that are still alive today, three—those of India, China, and the Islamic world—have retained this basic religious stamp down to our own time, while it is only in the course of the last few centuries that even our Western culture has largely dispensed with it.

On the basis of this identity of religion and culture, the High Civilizations brought to systematic completion the identification of human existence with the organic unity, power, and providence of nature and its vital rhythms. At the center of their organic world picture stood their conception of the creation of the world, an event that they conceived in the most varied forms: as a rising of the world out of the original waters; as the struggle of a god against the dragon of chaos or the original sea; as the sacrifice and dismemberment, even the self-dismemberment, of a gigantic primal being. This original act of creation was equated with the yearly cycle of growth and death of the plant world, in which it annually renewed itself and therefore had to be annually re-enacted, reinforced, and confirmed with ceremonial processions and games. From this cornerstone of the New Year celebrations there extended throughout the year a deeply meaningful succession of mythical festivals within which each of the processes of nature and human life found its place.

Together with the elaboration of this mythological world picture, the High Civilizations developed the few sparsely characterized divinities of the primitive mythological culture into brilliant groups of sharply individualized god-figures: gods of the universe, creation, and destruction, of the combative element in nature and man; gods of the heavens and the stars, the water, the rain, the floods, the sea; goddesses of Mother Earth and her fertility; gods of vegetation and the animal world; gods of every human activity. These manifold god-figures were then combined into the most varied orders as divine genealogies, assemblies, and even political communities of gods.

The growth of the particular spirit and outlook that characterizes each of the High Civilizations—and, similarly, the lesser civilizations that grew up around them—represents one of the most remarkable achievements in man's development of his powers. Just as each language has its peculiar spirit that intuitively guides those who speak it in their choice of words, idioms, and phrases, the particular aura of each of the High Civilizations tended to exercise the same guiding and organizing function. Each of them had its characteristic way of envisaging and shaping all its different expressions, from the forms of political organization through religion and the arts to the innermost thoughts of men. Those tendencies that were in tune with the general spirit of a civilization became a part of the pattern; those that ran counter to it remained unintegrated and were in time cast off.

The emergence of the High Civilizations also represented a decisive forward step in the development of man's distinctively human, political world. The unified planning and operation of the new hydraulic economy required a far more extensive and sophisticated administrative apparatus than that of the peasant village community. This then served to accentuate the gulf between leaders and led, between rulers and ruled, in a way that created sharp reciprocal tensions and was expressed and consolidated in the new political institution of the state. The separation and tension were all the sharper if—as may well have been the case—they resulted from the conquest and subjection of the peasant masses by warlike pastoral peoples in such a way that the fact of domination was reinforced by its alien character.

From their origins around 3000 B.C. down to the period of the First World War, the development of the High Civilizations is uniformly characterized by the institution of monarchical rule. The new tasks were so demanding, and the means of carrying them out were generally so limited, that only the most uncompromising concentration of all power in one hand offered a possibility of establishing and maintaining order and prosperity. Only as buffers between the larger and smaller empires and their dynasties do we find a few republics, mostly in the form of city-states. In the East their appearance is essentially limited to the earliest period of Mesopotamia and, here and there, in India. The unique development of our Western civilization was decisively influenced by the fact that here the predominance of the absolute ruler was much more sharply challenged and eventually overcome by the development of city-states.

The position of the ruler reflected his decisive significance in the structure of the High Civilizations. His greatness was felt to surpass all earthly power. He was himself a god, or the son of a god, or at least distinguished by a god's grace. His blood was not like that of other mortals. In addition to its immense stabilizing force, this concept of rulership based entirely on the person of the ruler and his royal house brought with it such negative features as the constant struggles for succession and the harem intrigues that continued in the Oriental dynasties down to the beginning of our century. For the plenary power of the single ruler could not be assured and, at the same time, limited in any kind of legal form. Individual rulership no doubt developed at an early stage an ethic of its own in the idea of a fatherly solicitude for the country—the ruler as the shepherd of his flock. But in spite of its ideals and the long series of really significant rulers who ceaselessly endeavored to realize them in practice, the monarchies of the agricultural civilization nevertheless remained basically unlimited and thus in constant danger of degenerating into mere despotism.

The result was that really fateful process which for five thousand years governed the ups and downs of the dynasties, at least the Oriental ones, like the play of waves on the sea. Some man with extraordinary gifts of rulership would fight his way up to the position of founder of a new dynasty. Among his immediate successors his energy would at first continue to express itself. Then it would rapidly decline under their weaker heirs, who would progressively sink into idleness and luxury until at last the chaos of their disintegrating rule enabled some new pretender to supplant the existing dynasty with his own.

The limitations that law could not impose upon the plenary power of the absolute ruler were nevertheless imposed by circumstances. The extent of their dominions surpassed by far the scope of their administrative means. True, the rulers of the High Civilizations were able to develop extensive networks of officials with bureaucratic rules, careers, and hierarchies. In the art of writing they developed a priceless aid for the communication of orders, the recording of facts, and the accumulation of official documents. But real control of this bureaucratic apparatus in the long run proved impossible. Even if an outstanding ruler succeeded in enforcing his will in the remotest corners of his empire, the reins immediately fell from the hands of his successors. The officials sent out to the provinces established themselves in their official seats, married into the local landed families, and consolidated themselves into a feudal nobility. Below the ruler and his official apparatus there were no elements that could have effectively redressed the balance.

The disparity of aims and means that characterized the political institutions of the High Civilizations was equally characteristic of their entire structure. Their soaring ideas everywhere transcended the means for their accomplishment. The High Civilizations simply lacked the internal strength needed for continuous, consistent advance. Periods of progress, often spectacular, were repeatedly cut short by the inherent limitations of the material basis and ended in stagnation or complete disintegration. Thus it might easily appear to their participants as if the same organic rhythms of birth, growth, dying, and rebirth that governed the life of nature and the human individual were also valid for those most comprehensive of all human achievements, the world empires and the High Civilizations themselves. This concept did in fact continue to dominate the outlook of the Indian and Chinese civilizations. It was its abandonment in favor of a more dynamic concept, in Judaism and in Greek and Roman antiquity, that prepared the way for the emergence of our Western civilization—a completely new High Civilization that was to diverge radically from all the others and would increasingly transcend their common horizon.

Man Outgrows the Mythological World

In the course of the first millennium B.C., the parallel development of the four main branches of mankind came to a parting of the ways. The two Eastern civilizations, India and China, experienced an intensification of their spiritual energies, a renewal and deepening of their motive impulses that was to maintain them as living entities down into our own time. Egypt and Mesopotamia did not experience a similar spiritual rebirth. Their energies became exhausted around 600 B.C. The process of civilization that they had inaugurated was nevertheless carried forward, though on sharply divergent lines, by the rise of monotheism in the Biblical tradition and the development of a secular civilization in Greece and Rome.

These two different traditions, the Biblical and the Graeco-Roman, together represent the second main phase in the story of Western civilization during the agricultural era. In the Roman Empire, both of them combined to form the new synthesis that was to be perfected in medieval Christendom—which, in turn, would give rise in the Renaissance to the modern civilization of the West. Whereas in the East we find two continuous High

Civilizations that run parallel throughout their entire course, in the West we are thus confronted with no less than four separate stages. The original mythological civilizations of Egypt and Mesopotamia are followed in the second stage by the emergence of two different world systems, the Biblical and the Graeco-Roman. The third stage, the Middle Ages, sees the union and interpenetration of these two traditions with the fresh energies of the northern, barbarian peoples; and finally, in the fourth stage, there comes the disruption of that union and the emergence of a wholly new way of life in the beginning of the modern era.

The event that brought about this radical separation between East and West was nothing else than a decisive advance in the development of spiritual power as it affected man's way of apprehending his world. From the mythological conception of a universe of many powers that had found expression in the High Civilizations, men now advanced to the notion of a single power which had created the world and all its elements and continued to sustain and influence it. But this confrontation with inherited mythological conceptions was carried through in fundamentally different ways by the civilizations of the Oriental and the Western groups. In the Indian and Chinese High Civilizations, the mythological cosmologies were preserved in radically deepened form. The Biblical and Greek cultures, on the other hand, pushed beyond this point to a radical break with any mythological limitations whatsoever. The result was a decisive liberation of the individual from all mythologically determined relationships, his establishment for the first time as an essentially independent being, and a new emphasis on his unique significance in this individual status.

The Chinese and Indian Cosmic Systems

In India and China, as we have indicated, the struggle with the original mythological religious systems did not result in any such clear-cut break. The old gods and demons were not repudiated but remained as objects of veneration and magic practices for the masses and, in sublimating reinterpretations, even for the elect. At the same time there grew up within these mythological conceptions new systems of philosophical speculation that endeavored to explain the world as the work of a single and universal world principle or life force, whose different elements were no longer the manifestations of different gods but the expressions of a single supreme, all-comprehensive principle.

In China this single ruling principle appears as the Tao, or the Way. But it was in India, which of all the High Civilizations has always shown the most remarkable gift for cosmic speculation, that the idea of a supreme ruling force was most fully developed. Since the time of the Upanishads (from 800 B.C.), Indian thought had reached beyond the gods to the notion of the Brahman as an all-powerful vital force, the ultimate source of all that exists, above and beyond all those distinctions we perceive at the human level between creative and destructive forces, between beneficial and awe-inspiring powers, between male and female, and even between good and evil. Everything that exists as a dynamic expression of life is held to be justified, true, and good by the mere fact of its existence.

In its inexhaustible drive toward realization, the Brahman constantly streams forward with ever-new strength and pours itself out in a bewildering multitude of special forms—gods, demons, men, animals, plants, mountains, rivers, seas—all of which are considered as so many different manifestations of the ultimate life force. All of them are interconnected and interchangeable. The world is not a hierarchy of static facts but a cosmos of processes. Everything evolves within itself, or transforms itself into something else. These processes are regulated by immutable laws. Once a process has been started, it must run its course to the end. Nothing can stop it; nothing gets lost on the way. As the final goal, beyond these innumerable transformations upward and downward, there shines forth the ultimate conquest of the drive toward realization itself and the return into the undifferentiated unity of the Brahman.

These comprehensive and sweeping cosmic conceptions left their imprint upon the formation of the human world as well. A single order seemed to govern heaven and earth, nature and culture, according to the same unvarying laws. The human world, that of culture, was seen not as separated and set in contrast to surrounding nature, but as being embedded in nature as one of her special expressions. Its cells were either natural biological communities, like the family, or could easily be regarded as such organic communities, as in the village, the guild, the relationship of teacher and student. Just as the Indian cosmology was distinguished by the conception of an all-comprehensive, all-inclusive change of forms, so the Indian social universe was stamped by its terrestrial counterpart, the caste system. Originally designed to separate different conquering and conquered races and to effect a separation and organic coexistence of different activities, the caste system became the powerful clamp which, even without political unity, held the Indian social world together for thousands of years.

Within this all-embracing network of cosmically sanctioned relationships, the individual could not possibly break through to the consciousness of his unique, particular self. Essentially he remained a member of the community that surrounded him. His aim could be only to accommodate himself to that larger unity and thus incorporate himself in the total harmony of the universe. His self-realization could be accomplished only in the form of self-subordination, in understanding and mastering himself within the social and cosmic orders. His highest ambition was to efface his personal individuality and merge himself once again in the flow of the world process.

This double consolidation, by a comprehensive cosmology and a corresponding social structure, is largely responsible for the amazing consistency and durability that enabled both the Indian and the Chinese civilizations to outlive by so many centuries their Egyptian and Mesopotamian counterparts. Admittedly, however, this very consistency was a fatal obstacle to their further development. The unity and harmony that characterized their world pictures led both Indians and Chinese to look upon them as something fundamentally and eternally valid. And, though these cosmologies were of a kind that left ample room for the further elaboration and refinement of the two cultures, they did not admit of the kind of internal development that could at some point have fundamentally disrupted the cosmologies themselves.

The Biblical Tradition

In contrast to the Oriental High Civilizations of India and China, whose struggles with the mythological world picture resulted in its preservation in a philosophically deepened and cosmically elaborated form, both the Biblical tradition and Greek civilization arrive at a complete victory over the mythological outlook and a complete reaffirmation of the individual in his unique significance. They arrive at this result in opposite ways, however: in the Biblical tradition, through the consolidation and deepening of the underlying religious feeling; in Greek civilization, through a break with any religious bondage and the assertion of a completely secular attitude.

The Biblical tradition derives its unique and radical conception of the world and man from the desert in which it was formed and from which it comes to us, clear, sharp, sober, passionate, uncompromising. It was this spirit that sustained the people of Israel as, after bitter enslavement and prolonged wandering, they fought their way into the Promised Land and thus entered into the completely different environment of the Palestinian peasantry, with its sensuous cults, its ecstatic rites, its fertility orgies, its child sacrifices, and its multiplicity of local divinities on every hill and at every well. From their entry into the Promised Land until their banishment, the life of the people of Israel becomes a single, uninterrupted, life-and-death struggle with the seductions of this strange world—a struggle in which the quite different basis of their own religious feeling comes to be ever more deeply illuminated and more sharply forged and elaborated.

This basic religious feeling has its root in the belief in Jehovah as the one God—at first the God of *the* People, later of all peoples. In contrast to India and China, the break with the multitudinous nature gods of the polytheistic religions is completely uncompromising. For Israel, there is simply God. God appears as a being beyond and above the world, completely independent within Himself. God simply is. When Moses asks God how he shall name Him to the children of Israel, God answers: "I AM THAT I AM. . . . Thus shalt thou say unto the children of Israel, I AM hath sent me unto you." (Exod. 3:14.)

As Absolute Being or Reality, God is Absolute Power, Absolute Creativity. God does not, like the supra-personal Brahman, pour out His divine substance upon a world which is only an emanation of Himself and which He eventually takes back into Himself. God creates the world as something different from Himself. He creates it "out of nothing." He creates it as something that, for all its imperfections and deficiencies, is fundamentally valuable and significant in itself. Above all, God is not, like the Tao or the Brahman, a principle or life force. God is a person. He is not merely all-powerful, but above all, He is moral force, moral concern. God is not, as in the Oriental religions, a being aloof from good and evil. He is passionately concerned with good and evil— passionately affirming the one, passionately rejecting the other. This concern with moral values, with justice, is the very essence of His character. God is a person, because only a person is capable of feeling this intimate concern with justice.

The intensely personal character of the God of the Biblical tradition determines man's own position in a quite new way. Man is no longer, as in the Oriental cosmologies, an insignificant part of the cosmos, a mere fleeting manifestation in the flow of the world order. As a person fashioned in the image of God, man is, like God himself, raised out of the world. He has been freed by God from the bondage of nature and separated from her, even set above her. He was created out of nature in order that he might rule over nature. Thus the Biblical tradition presents the first cosmology in which man is defined not in terms of his humanness, of his being rooted in nature, but in terms of his radical separation from nature and his intrinsic superiority to nature.

In sharp contrast to the Eastern teachings, therefore, man's morality does not consist simply in realizing and fulfilling his role within the cosmos. It consists quite specifically in obeying God's commands. Beyond everything else, man's role on earth is to seek to fulfill God's supreme concern with justice and morality, particularly when God's moral demands involve him in a conflict with the natural impulses of his animal body and soul. It is in asserting his spiritual and moral self in this basic conflict with the animal roots of his nature that an individual becomes truly a person.

Such a conquest of man's animal impulses in obedience to God is not brought about by any single effort. It involves a conflict within the person himself, one that must be fought out over and over again. This struggle, moreover, concerns not only the individual but society, the people whom God has chosen as the bearers of His will. Thus the struggle against the fertility cults of the surrounding peoples, and, beyond that, against all forms of injustice, becomes a national mission—a mission that was recognized and carried forward by the Prophets as the protagonists of the painful inner development in which God's plan for His people comes to fulfillment.

As the Prophets one by one come forward to assume the crushing burden of mediating God's commands, there gradually emerges a completely new concept of human existence and its cosmic relationships. Instead of being incorporated in a cyclical universal process, as in the mythological cultures, the individual is now incorporated in a one-time, end-directed or teleological process: the development of the people of Israel, and eventually of all mankind, according to God's plan. In grasping and incorporating himself into this world plan, the individual passes from a world that is conceived essentially in a spatial manner into one that is essentially time-conceived.

At the same time, his basic orientation is changed from one of more or less passive adaptation to an omnipotent process into an active and responsible participation in a quite different process, one whose course is eternally threatened and doubtful and whose ultimate success remains dependent on his own personal participation. In taking upon himself this co-responsibility for the process set in motion by God's will, the individual involves himself in an inescapable tension between his conception of this process as it formed itself in the past, his solemn responsibility for its continuance through his own decisions in the present, and the always uncertain outlook for its continuation in the future. Here, in this threefold development within the Biblical tradition, originates the concept of history.

The development set in motion by the Prophets of the Old Testament was to find its continuation and completion in Christianity. In it, God's solicitude, originally limited to His Chosen People, is extended to embrace all peoples. His passionate demand for justice broadens into His inexhaustible love. The prophetic mission of self-realization through self-conquest, originally the mission of a chosen few, becomes the task of everyone. In the place of care for the justice of God, which is difficult but not fundamentally unattainable, there appears in the Christian consciousness of guilt a feeling of the radical and incurable insufficiency of the individual self. With this feeling there appears in the soul of each individual a never-to-be-conquered tension that forbids him to find peace within himself and compels him to demand from himself, in ceaseless exertion, the maximum of which he is capable.

Greek Civilization

If the unique achievement of the Biblical tradition was the shattering of the mythological world picture through a total concentration of its basic religious feeling in the person of the living God, the unique achievement of Greek civilization was precisely the opposite. It, too, involved a shattering of the mythological cosmology, but this time as a step toward the radical secularization of culture. Culture, as the unfolding of a sense of life that is no longer religious but completely secularized, is the real discovery of the Greeks.

Like the people of Israel, the Greeks on their irruption into the Aegean world came under the spell of a far more advanced mythological culture, that of Crete. The first wave of Greek invaders in the Achaean and Mycenaean period succumbed so completely to this culture that its representatives can hardly be said to belong to Greek civilization in the true sense. When the curtain rises again after the centuries of darkness that followed the destruction of the Cretan-Mycenaean culture by the invading sea peoples, the break with the original mythological religion has already been carried through. The new Greek world belonged to the new Olympian gods. Those elements that survived from the earlier religious stratum were partly incorporated into the Olympian circle, like Dionysus, and in part continued to exist side by side with the latter, as in the Eleusinian mysteries and the Orphic cults—though without occasioning such passionate conflicts as those between Jehovah and Baal and Moloch, and without calling in question the decisive position of the new gods.

As gods, the Olympian divinities play a peculiar dual role in the development of Greek civilization. They represent, at one and the same time, both the embodiment of a mythological world picture and the decisive step away from it. On one side they remain the expression of a true mythological feeling, even a comparatively primitive one that has neither arrived at philosophical clarification, as in India and China, nor undergone a real religious transfiguration, as in Israel. In this sense they are the legitimate religious representatives of the new Greek people, by and through whom this new people becomes conscious of its cultural unity even without having gone through the process of political unification. Yet at the same time this religious feeling, having failed to consolidate itself into any one of the higher stages attained in other civilizations, has in an inward sense already reached its end

with the Olympians themselves. They are still wholly gods, and
at the same time they are really gods no longer.

Conceived in the form of oversized human beings, the Olympian gods are undoubtedly figures of unique intellectual attrac-
tiveness and aesthetic charm; yet they are without any real inner
consistency. With their purely human forms they lack the truly
godlike qualities, the supernaturally mysterious, the weightiness
of supernatural reality. And, since their superior power in relation
to men could be made clear only by freeing them from the specifically human weaknesses, trouble and toil, pain and sorrow and
death, they also lack the gravity of human existence, its characteristic seriousness. Their superiority to men remains a pure superiority of power, pure caprice without justice, without fidelity even
toward their own favorites. And this superiority is also incapable
of radiating any sense of obligation.

The Olympian gods thus represent a peculiar transitional form
that, by its very nature, was bound to lead eventually to internal
dissolution. As figures, nevertheless, they are not only the first real
manifestation of the Greek spirit but also the point of departure
from which the Greek mind could advance from the liquidation
of its religious world picture to the construction of a new and
purely secular one. In creating the individual gods, each of them
a concrete and plastic embodiment of a whole field of existence,
the Greeks revealed the unique richness of their imagination as
well as their extreme sensitivity to the sensuous aspect of the
world's manifestations, a sensitivity that sometimes went almost
to the length of completely ignoring its real essence. Yet this total
surrender to appearances was accompanied by an equally complete detachment from them, a completely unprejudiced way of
looking at things and an ability suddenly to perceive behind the
sensuous appearances their innermost essence and interrelationship. An interesting progression leads from the concrete conception of the Olympian gods in Homer's epic, through the
personified abstractions, such as Dike, Themis, Mnemosyne, as we
find them above all in Hesiod, to the central concern of Greek phi-

losophy, the cosmos as the sensuous conception of the entire universe in its essential interrelatedness.

With their advance from conceiving the world in the persons of the Olympian gods to its conception as a rationally ordered cosmos, the Greeks accomplished a break with the mythologically limited world picture of the High Civilizations that in its own way was no less decisive than that of the Biblical tradition. Where the breakthrough of the Bible led to belief in the living God, that of the Greeks led to the development of secular culture and to philosophy. And, in contrast to the Biblical tradition, where the political and social structure remained largely intact, the Greeks in their emergence from the mythological world effected a corresponding advance on the political and social plane as well. Parallel to the breakthrough from *mythos* to *logos,* from the Olympian gods to the cosmos, there ran a breakthrough from the aristocratic society of early Greek times to the city-state, the *polis,* of the classical period.

The aristocratic society of pre-classical Greece is without a parallel in the entire development of the High Civilizations. As a transitional form that grew up amid the collapse of the Mycenaean great kingship and the chaos of the period of Greek migrations, it exactly corresponds to the transitional position of the Olympian gods. As a form of rulership, it represents the extreme of looseness and disintegration, a situation almost of anarchy in which the powerful noble families held the reins and exercised their power according to quite personal considerations in a network of friendships, feuds, and party alliances that crisscrossed the slowly consolidating landscape in every direction.

This very loose political organization was the expression of a boundless feeling for life, a passionate emphasis on the self and on one's own strength, a compulsion to exercise this strength, to test it against dangers of all kinds and thus win what stood above everything else for this aristocratic society—honor. This passionate emphasis on one's own strength, this unrestrained assertion of one's own will, worth, and self formed the essence of the Greek aristocratic outlook. It gave to this society a special element of harshness, of unrestrained ambition in the pursuit of one's own advantage, of extreme sensitivity toward any impairment of one's own dignity, of implacable hatred against the adversary, of readiness to suffer destruction rather than give way, which the other, pleasanter aspects of the Greek character—its outgoingness and generosity, its sense of propriety and accessibility to everything intellectual—transfigured to some extent but did not really soften. The Olympian gods, in their naked power, their lack of any sense of obligation, were only the projections of this aristocratic attitude. Whereas in the Biblical tradition the striving for self-realization found its expression in self-conquest, in the Greek civilization it expresses itself through the most unlimited development of the individual personality.

This aristocratic and secular feeling for life did not end with the passing of the aristocratic society of early Greek times but was in due course transmitted to the new political and social order of the city-state. Even more than the aristocratic society, the *polis* is a structure unique in the development of man. What it represented was the transference of the passionate Greek urge toward public life, public existence and activity, toward honor, from the individual to the society as a whole. In other words, it represented a grouping together of individuals into a community wholly oriented toward public existence, public actions and creations. In the aristocratic society, the individual urge toward distinction and honor had caused this public aspect to be thrust aside and more or less lost amid a network of private relationships, efforts, and rivalries. In the *polis,* on the other hand, this collective urge led to the strongest conceivable consolidation of public life and the most uncompromising subordination to it of all private strivings and interests.

For the Greek of the classical period, his *polis* was everything—and it demanded everything from him. It was a political community that gave him the opportunity to influence his own fate through participation in its affairs; a legal community that protected him against despotic caprice; a defense community that guarded him against external dangers; a place for the cultivation of all the varieties of physical and intellectual development; the scene of sociable or uplifting community life, in the market place, in competitions, processions, and cults; not least, a large family in which everyone knew everyone else. In return for all this, the *polis* demanded a complete surrender of the individual to its prosperity and greatness, a willing sacrifice of time, strength, fortune, and, when necessary, life. For the Greek, the city-state was more than an all-inclusive community; it was the real content of life. This secular society became the basis of life in a sense that hitherto only religions had been.

In its ruthless subordination of all private and individual claims to the overriding demands of the public interest, the Greek *polis* offered one extreme solution to a problem that was beginning to loom increasingly large in the development of Western civilization. This was the problem of the balance or correlation between public and private interests, between the rights and claims of the public and private "spheres." The extremist character of the Greek solution to this perennial problem will become more evident as we contemplate the alternative pattern of state and society that was meanwhile developing in ancient Rome.

The Romans

Beside the Greeks, the Romans stand as a second main element in the development of ancient civilization. In spite of fundamental similarities with the Greeks, they are the exponents of a culture that is entirely individual in character and, in its essential features, the very opposite of the Hellenic civilization.

Both civilizations, the Greek and the Roman, were ruled and stamped by their noble classes. But in contrast to the knightly aristocracy of the Greeks—greathearted, freehanded, passionately addicted to fighting and the chase, uniquely accessible to everything intellectual and artistic, yet flawed by untamable ambition and careless frivolity, moody and unstable—the Roman nobility was and remained a highly bred peasantry, with a simplicity and sobriety that was thoroughly practical and realistic in character—economical, even miserly, with a deep feeling for security; ready for war when it seemed unavoidable, but by no means seeking it; fundamentally averse to hunting, as to everything intellectual and artistic; cautious, stable, and unshakably reliable. Where the Greeks, with all their shortcomings and vices, have an irresistible attraction for us because of their sparkling genius, their incomparable gift for intellectual penetration, their unlimited openheartedness, the Romans are more likely to repel us, at first, by their awkwardness and shyness about expressing their real nature. Unlike the Greeks, they reveal themselves only laboriously and step by step under patient and sympathetic scrutiny.

In order to understand the unique achievements of the Roman civilization, one must realize that the sobriety of the Romans does not spring from any flat rationality, any lack of intellectual energies or spiritual qualities. On the contrary, wherever we enter into the life of the Roman people, we find it overflowing with spiritual energies: modesty before the gods, respect for parents and superiors, the passionate ambition of the great aristocratic families, the hearty life of the family circle, the feeling for the morally binding forces of mutual obligation in all the forms of human coexistence. The Romans' special significance lies precisely in their intensive understanding of these irrational elements and bonds; in their sense for what has developed and grown organically, rather than merely sprung from abstract thought; for moral, as contrasted with merely formal, obligations; in their reliance on tradition, experience, instinct. If the world-historical achievement of the Greeks lies in the discovery and development of man's rational powers, that of the Romans lies in having intuitively grasped and formed the irrational forces of the human endowment and of human existence.

Characteristically, this was done not in the Greek manner, in brilliant intellectual constructions and sharply defined abstract theories, but implicitly, in the practical elaboration of concrete

forms of community life. The underlying concept whose obligations govern the entire life of Roman society—that of the *mos
majorum,* the manners and customs of the ancestors—is no abstract
rule, but rather the living example of the ancestors as presented
in concrete figures and situations by a Brutus, Camillus, or Corio-
lanus. This ancestral example binds the feelings through veneration, convinces the practical sense by its concrete character, offers
a guide and model for later generations, and governs the forms
and organs of both public and private life in their competence
and operation.

The way of the ancestors continues throughout as the Romans'
guiding model. Every innovation had to be legitimized by invok-
ing it. Yet what we are here concerned with is no hollow, mechanical tradition such as suffocates one's own spiritual forces. It
is a living sense of association with the continuing life force of
one's own past. As such, it serves to promote the organic continuation of this force and its flexible adaptation to new conditions
even while the original forms appear to be preserved. It represents, so to speak, the spiritual clamp that held the Roman people
together in their development through time.

In the center of this development stands the problem of power,
of the struggle for power among the aristocratic families, and of
its regulation and control. The Romans were one-sidedly oriented
toward power to a degree that we encounter in almost no other
people. Not, however, in the sense of that unlimited personal
striving for power which we find in the great Greek power-figures
—and not in the sense of that objective affirmation of power as a
necessary law unto itself which Machiavelli derived from Livy at
the beginning of the modern era. The Romans grasped the nature
of power intuitively, and precisely because they did this with
their instinct and not with their intellect, they grasped not only
the nature of power but also its limitations, those that were set
by the equal striving for power of others and those necessitated by
the common benefit of all.

This concept of power, and, concurrently, of the limitations of power, found its classic expression in that most fundamental and characteristically Roman creation, the *res publica*. The *res publica,* the commonwealth, the embodiment of the common interest of all citizens, is something independent in itself, a supreme authority that absolutely transcends the desires and interests of the individual citizens and to which the latter are unconditionally subordinated. Thus it can serve at one and the same time as the arena of the struggle for power and the ambitions of individuals—or, rather, of the great aristocratic families—and as a sharply drawn boundary against the unrestricted pursuit of these ambitions.

The Roman's will to power finds its fulfillment in the magistracy, which, because it is conducted in the interest of the *res publica,* is invested with an almost absolute plenitude of power that is subjected to only a few limitations in the course of Rome's historical development. Yet this apparently unlimited power of the magistracy is in reality limited from the most varied directions: through the collegial form, at least in principle, of all offices, with the single exception of the dictatorship; through the authority of the Senate, whose counsel the official is bound to seek, and which he cannot disregard without very serious grounds; and through the popular assembly. Above all, it is limited by a completely unwritten element, the inner obligation of all Romans and of the magistrate in particular to the *res publica*. The thought of setting oneself against the *res publica,* as the great contenders for power among the Greeks so often set themselves against their *polis,* does not occur to the Romans. Their history knows no traitor to his country, and the few attempts at violent internal revolution immediately encountered the strongest resistance.

Two elements thus stand side by side in the *res publica:* the good of the community and the striving for power of the individual. They do not, however, confront each other in unrelated hostility; nor do they stand in any merely mechanical equilibrium. They are related to each other in a reciprocal tension in which each element justifies the other and brings it to fulfillment. The *res publica* gives the magistrate his office, with its plenitude of power; the magistrates, on their side, represent, maintain, and defend the *res publica,* the common weal, by their activity. It is characteristic, moreover, that the two elements of this tension do not meet on the same plane, and are not of equal weight and value. The *res publica* remains clearly superior to the magistrate, however much it depends on him for its representation and defense.

This peculiar situation of the *res publica,* as a tension in which the common weal is definitely superior to its various individual elements, repeats itself and is further clarified in another, similar situation of tension that formed the basis of the whole structure of Roman society: the relationship between *res publica* and *res privata,* between the public and the private spheres. In contrast to the Greeks, whose feeling for life was completely fulfilled in a one-sided surrender to their *polis,* the life of the Roman people in all its branches rests on a carefully maintained relationship between *res publica* and *res privata.* The public religion, or better, the public cults of the state gods, are matched by the private cults of the tribal and family gods. The unlimited power of the *res publica* over all citizens in matters affecting the common advantage is matched by the equally unlimited *patria potestas,* the power of the father of the household over all who are subjected to it. The public possessions of the state are matched by the Roman conception of the *dominium,* the mastery of the property owner over his land and property.

This state of affairs has given rise to the erroneous impression that the relationship between public and private areas, between state and family, involves merely the juxtaposition of two spheres that stand side by side with equal rights, and on which Roman existence rests as on two pillars. But if we look closely, we discover that here, too, it is a case not of juxtaposition but of a tension, and not of equal rights but of a superiority of one to the other. The *res publica* is not the equal of the *res privata,* but is unconditionally superior to it. However anxiously the *res publica* endeavored to leave the regulation of private affairs to private self-help, it would never have occurred to a Roman to doubt its basic right to intervene in the private sphere in case the interests of the community demanded it.

Indeed, such intervention regularly took place in the exercise of that most characteristically Roman institution, the censorship, which was responsible for periodically reviewing and bringing up to date the list of citizens. In judging the moral attitude of the individual citizens, the censors took into account not only the proper fulfillment of their public duties but also their private life insofar as it could in any way arouse justified objections. And their censure invariably had serious political, social, and even material consequences for the person affected. From the standpoint of its impact on the *res publica,* individual conduct was definitely regarded as a matter of public concern even where no specific legal transgression was involved.

As compared with the Greeks' subordination to the *polis,* the great achievement of the Romans consisted precisely in the way in which they built up the life of their people on the well-balanced interrelationship of the two spheres so that each was assured of its own integrity and emphasis; while at the same time their interdependence and, within it, the pre-eminence in principle of the public over the private sphere were also assured. With their unique sense for the requirements of human coexistence, the Romans were the first to recognize that in the long run it was impossible to tolerate either an unclear association of public and private existence, as in the Oriental civilizations, or a one-sided emphasis on the public such as the Greeks attempted, but that what was needed was a clear-cut demarcation of a private sphere within the public one. They further saw that this demarcation could not be carried out mechanically, but would inevitably raise the problem of the relationship and interdependence between the two; and they resolved this problem with an intuitive sureness by establishing the superiority in principle of the public over the private sphere. Thus their work became a "treasure for all times." While the *polis* shone out in the development of mankind as a splendidly colored meteor and then disappeared forever, the development of the *res publica* and the regulation of the relationship between public and private spheres laid the foundations for the development of the modern state.

THE IMPACT OF CHRISTIANITY

The heritage that Rome bequeathed to later times included not only the secular culture of the ancient world—the creations of the Greek genius in philosophy, science, and art and those of the Roman in the spirit and forms of community life and law—but also the religious tradition of the Bible with its belief in the one God, its conception of man as God's counterpart, as a being with a unique responsibility toward God and toward history, and its radical opposition to the secular tradition with its basis in philosophy. Because of the dispersion and internal divisions of Judaism, however, this Biblical religious tradition was not passed on in its entirety of unity and contradiction but only as it had been transformed in Christianity.

The Christian Revolt

As an offshoot of Judaism, Christianity inevitably stood in a somewhat ambivalent relationship to its Jewish root. In one sense, the division did not signify any absolute separation or radical recommencement. Even after its severance from Judaism, Christianity still retained the Old Testament as the basis of faith, though with a different and self-oriented interpretation. On the other hand, the severance did amount to a radical break rather than a simple continuation "in a new key." In an external sense, this was an inevitable result of Christ's condemnation and execution as a heretic and of the subsequent exclusion of the original Christian community by Jewish orthodoxy. But it also represented an inward rupture that grew out of the complete disavowal by Christianity of the two main elements of Jewish belief: the idea of the Chosen People and the central emphasis on the justice of the law. This relationship of simultaneous affirmation and opposition toward Judaism introduced into the new Christianity at its very outset a tension that was to be of decisive importance in its further development as well as in its encounter with the Graeco-Roman tradition and the youthful forces of the northern peoples.

A basically ambivalent relationship to the Jewish tradition is found from the very beginning in Jesus himself. It is true that His work was begun entirely within the framework of the Jewish tradition. Far from contesting the validity of this tradition, He expressly emphasizes that He has come not to destroy the law and the Prophets, but to fulfill them. Even His contradiction of the tradition was linked to it in the sense that it represented a resumption of the protest of the Prophets which had contributed so decisively to its formation. But this comparison with the Prophets reveals most clearly the point at which Jesus' own protest unavoidably brought Him into conflict with the tradition itself.

For the protest of the Prophets had been basically directed against completely unambiguous and open offenses—the confusion of burnt offerings with piety; the denial of justice to the weak and oppressed; disobedience by kings and rulers to the will of God. In the Judaism of His time, Jesus is no longer confronted in any serious degree with this type of unambiguous offense. On the contrary, this people, which God's hand had mercifully led back out of exile, was proudly aware of its chosenness and passionately striving to show itself worthy of this status by the most extreme demonstration of faithfulness to God and His law. Its whole ambition and effort were directed toward conducting this new life in a manner pleasing to God. It thus surrounded its whole existence with a network of commands, and especially prohibitions, which were made continuously more comprehensive and more difficult to fulfill by the constant addition of ever more sharply thought-out refinements. Enthusiasm for the law and its fulfillment was raised to the level of a real virtuosity.

Precisely here, however, lay the germ of an infinitely deeper, infinitely more serious disobedience to God than the open offenses against His commandments. Not only did this dissolution of man's obedience to God into a matter of carrying out a complex system of commands and prohibitions involve the individual in a most unedifying casuistry, especially in the central point of Sabbath observance. It also meant that the original concept of obedience to God's will was transformed into a purely legal relationship in which the inner obligation was formalized and externalized, in which external correctness could go hand in hand with a quite impure will. It tended to seduce a man into the belief that he could legally reckon up his fulfillment of this system of commands vis-à-vis God, that he could even completely fulfill his duty and obligation to God and achieve a position of "justification" toward Him. Worst of all, such self-complacency could lead to a form of self-glorification in which the just man would feel entitled to look down "pharisaically" on his less just fellow men. The danger was that the seductions of this psychology of law and reward would lead unnoticed to the most profound hardening of the heart. And this danger was all the greater because, in contrast to open offense, it remained entirely invisible.

It is precisely here that Jesus launches his attack. Confronted with this phenomenon of disobedience disguised as fulfillment of the law, injustice disguised as justice, arrogance disguised as humility, He sets out at the very beginning to uncover the contradiction and bring it to light. Against this mock justice, which lays so much stress on the law and its scrupulous fulfillment, Jesus goes back to the source of this law in the living will of God, whose expression it is, after all, supposed to be.

This living will of God is invoked by Jesus not in the traditional preaching in the synagogue but in the midst of daily life, amid the familiar scenes of His Galilean homeland and in encounters with men of the most varied types. His teaching springs not from a general rule but is, in every instance, directly derived from a concrete situation. It seizes upon the hearer, often without any preliminaries, with the direct question, "Which of you?"—

thus seeking to overcome his detachment, involve him directly in the situation, and force him to ask himself what he himself would do in similar circumstances.

In this direct appeal to the individual to place himself in the given situation and decide for the living will of God in opposition to all conventional conceptions and rules, Jesus goes straight to the basic problem of all human existence—the fact, namely, that while all social coexistence necessarily demands order, this order, being secular in character, is bound to remain deficient, rigid, and unjust and must inevitably involve the individual in an insoluble conflict between its formal demands and his obedience to the will of God. This conflict between worldly existence and God's rule and will is inescapable, and must be sustained even when it seems to the individual that the gulf between his capacity and God's will is hopelessly wide.

Yet the readiness for a struggle that Jesus keeps on demanding does not mean complete devaluation of this world, but rather a proper relationship to the world, an inner detachment from it. Uncompromising as His demands are in principle, He himself shows in His parables the deepest and liveliest understanding for this world with its large and small joys and sorrows. He takes part without embarrassment in its good gifts, and is in consequence derided by His opponents as a glutton and drunkard, a wastrel and a winebibber. His doctrine not only speaks anger against the unjust and the hypocrites, but is also illuminated by joy and cheerfulness.

The message of Jesus, thus, is paradoxical through and through. It is not by chance that this is so, nor is it simply because He found in paradox an especially effective method of fixing and holding His hearers' attention. It is paradoxical from the deepest inner necessity, from the very nature of the things it is concerned with. It is paradoxical because the tension between the conventional, apparent order of the world and its real order according to the will of God is itself a unique and tremendous paradox and, as such, can be grasped, sustained, and overcome only in paradoxical form.

It was, in all probability, precisely this paradoxical element in Jesus' teaching that led the scribes and Pharisees to regard His radical appeal from the letter of the law to its spirit as a revolutionary attack on the law itself and on their entire world. It is true that His basic demands, the emphasis on belief as opposed to compliance with the law, and on the love of one's neighbor as the highest command, were in no way foreign to Jewish religious thinkers. For them, however, such concepts remained within the framework of the law itself; in a sense they represented its peaceful crowning. The revolutionary explosive force with which Jesus invested them was quite another matter, and created an unbridgeable opposition that He himself was the first to recognize. Thus His journey to Jerusalem, undertaken in order to force the people to make a decisive choice, led with inexorable necessity to His arrest, trial for heresy, and crucifixion.

It is precisely at this moment, when Jesus' painful and ignominious death appears to have put out the flame He had lighted, that the miracle occurs. The unheard-of miracle of the Resurrection, authenticated by a large number of reliable witnesses, becomes the rock on which His scattered and perplexed disciples reassemble and found their community. In consequence, His teaching is not simply continued but deepened and radically transformed. Belief in His teachings now becomes fundamentally a belief in Jesus himself, in His individual identity. The salvation of all who acknowledge and believe in Him becomes the fundamental and central fact of the new religion.

This change of emphasis became all the more decisive as the meaning attributed to Jesus himself was deepened and broadened. For the original Christian community, Jesus' resurrection portended more than anything else God's own acknowledgment of One to whom this world had denied its acknowledgment, whom it had condemned, and to whom even His own disciples had not remained faithful. The Messianic expectations that had surrounded Him in the eyes of His disciples were crystallized by the miracle of the Resurrection into the rock-ribbed conviction that He had been not only the man they had known but, in very truth, by God's own witness, God's own Son. The historically verified fact of the Resurrection also guaranteed for them the supra-historical fact of Jesus' position as the Son of God, His becoming flesh and His transfiguration. It was through this fact that Jesus, if one may so express it, became Christ.

In the framework of this observation, which alone makes possible the understanding of Christianity in its special power and efficacy and in its relationship to other decisive movements of world history, it is neither necessary nor appropriate to pursue further this extension of the Christ-figure from the historical into the supra-historical realm. It is true that in doing so we should find ample confirmation of what has been said about the essentially paradoxical character of Christianity and its resultant unique elasticity and vitality. Here, however, instead of following the development of Christian belief and dogma, we must limit ourselves to examining the decisive steps in the development of the structure of Christian feeling and thought.

Christianity Becomes a World Movement

This further development was essentially the work of Paul, who, from being the most convinced defender of Jewish legal belief and the most violent persecutor of the new doctrine, became its most passionate and tireless apostle. Paul's intellectual confrontation with his own origins and development occurs in the most important of his Epistles, that to the Romans, especially in the seventh chapter. Significantly, its point of departure is no longer a mere contradiction within the law, between its letter and its spirit, but a fundamental contradiction in the conception of human nature itself.

Human nature, that is, the human will, was not a fundamental problem for Judaism. Man, according to the Jewish belief, had been created by God in His own image. That meant that man's will in itself was good, even though weak and contestable in accordance with his nature as a creature. Man was capable with his own strength of desiring good, of doing it, and thus of earning credit with God, even if he had to depend on God's mercy for his complete justification.

For Paul, this conception of human nature as essentially good is the basic error that leads to destruction. The fundamental observation from which he proceeds is not that of the natural goodness of the human will but of its natural perversity. The natural man, in his self-will and instinctive self-assertiveness, seemed to Paul to be hardened at his very roots and basically in revolt against God. Through this hardening, his will had so radically fallen a prey to evil that he was incapable even of desiring good, at least rightly desiring it, let alone doing it.

This radical obduracy and misdirection of the human will, which had come into the world with Adam's fall, was what Paul called guilt. It was man's guilt that enslaved him to the world and its powers, to the flesh, to sin and death. And this happened without man in his natural condition being in any way aware of his enslavement. Thus he could lull himself in the belief that he led his life with his own strength and could even earn justice in the eyes of God. In this belief that one can win justice before God through one's own strength, one's fulfillment of the law, and one's good works, there lies for Paul the real fundamental sin, the extreme of self-will and self-assertion.

Salvation from sin, in Paul's eyes, is possible for man only if instead of building on his own strength and fulfillment of the law, he decisively breaks and abandons his self-will, his urge to self-assertion. He must frankly admit his guilt and the complete perversity of his will. He must give up all self-justification and all boasting before God and must totally surrender himself to God's mercy, accepting the forgiveness of his guilt through the sacrificial death of Christ. Only in this way can he free himself from the world's bonds.

Thus Paul arrives at the same idea of total dependence on the will of God that had represented the heart of Jesus' own doctrine. Paul, too, takes upon himself the special relationship to the world that goes with this attitude, and that is neither a thoughtless surrender to the world nor a total devaluation but rather a right relationship to it, one that combines participation in its affairs with the maintenance of an inner detachment. And thus Paul's message, precisely in its wholehearted acceptance of unconditional guilt, is not dark and gloomy but joyful and sparkling with passionate love for his fellow men. Far from being an expression of weakness, it reflects unshakable inner strength, a wellspring of potency.

Paul's teaching concerning guilt and grace did not at first find any logical continuation within the powerfully swelling tide of Christianity. At first, in the conflict of the new religion with the secular inheritance of the ancient world, the Eastern Roman Empire with its common Greek language and its philosophical tradition stood centuries ahead of its Western counterpart. This Eastern, Greek branch of Christendom was so filled with the thought of the creation of man in God's image that the spoiling of human nature through sin seemed to it to be only a distortion, a contamination of the divine image rather than a radical perversion and guilt—an attitude that the Orthodox church has maintained down to our own day. In the passionate enthusiasm with which it received the gospel, Greek Christianity thus oriented itself entirely toward joy and jubilation, toward rebirth and new creation.

Meanwhile the Western, Latin branch, whose Roman way of thought was essentially much closer to the Pauline teaching in its emphasis on sobriety, discipline, and the practical shaping of community life, was still far too backward to be able to take advantage of so profound and far-reaching an analysis. Only with the flowering of Latin theology toward the end of the fourth century A.D. is Paul rediscovered and attention redirected to his central demand for belief as distinguished from law. This happens primarily through the man who was by far the most significant of all the church fathers, Augustine.

The Augustinian Synthesis

With Augustine we come to one of those decisive personalities of world history whose stature and significance continue to increase the more closely we examine them. It is not only the spell of his personality that still captivates us after so many centuries—the freshness, openness, and warmth of his nature, his uncompromising quest for truth. Nor is it the brilliance and multiplicity of his gifts as a master of language, profound student of the human soul, and practical guide of the church. It is primarily his astounding ability to turn and grow that determines the strangely involved course of his life and brings him, as it did Paul, to combine the fulfillment of his quite personal mission and destiny with the completion of the objective task of his time. This task was nothing less than the joining together of the basic elements of the Biblical and the Graeco-Roman inheritance.

We have seen that the Biblical tradition and Greek culture, each in its own fashion, had represented a decisive break with the mythological world pictures of the High Civilizations. In this process, each of them had developed common traits that sharply distinguish them from the two Eastern civilizations of India and China. Far from reducing man to a mere member of the universal order, they had set him on his own feet and emphasized his personal meaning. In contrast to the Eastern tendency toward compromise and mediation, they had developed a rationally clear-cut type of thinking that brought contrary concepts into high relief. In contrast to the Eastern tendency to allow events to develop, they had introduced an active, operational attitude.

Yet in spite of these common "Western" traits, the contrasts and contradictions between the two branches of Western culture remained extraordinarily great. Originating in basically different attitudes, they had developed their own radically different cosmologies or world pictures. The Biblical conception of the creation of the world out of nothing stood in flat contradiction to the Greek conception of the eternity of the world. The Biblical conception of the subsequent development of this world as a non-repetitive process conflicted with the Greek conception of recurrent cycles. The Biblical conception of man as an individual person conflicted with the Greek conception of man as representative of a type. Passion stood against reason, the striving for humility against the striving for honor; the Biblical ideal of realization through self-conquest was pitted against the Greek idea of self-development.

The reconciliation of these contradictions was bound to be an extremely difficult and long-continuing task. What was involved was not merely the tying together of the Christian religion with the secular culture of the Greeks. Rather it was a question of bringing into harmony two world pictures that radically contradicted each other at many fundamental points. Undoubtedly this unique contradictoriness of its foundations served to give Western civilization an extraordinary liveliness and scope. But it also made the conquest of these contradictions a task that could not be carried out all at once or once for all. Attempts to do so did not last. Sooner or later the various solutions broke down again as the original contradictions re-emerged.

It was in Augustine that the first great attempt at a fusion of these disparate elements, undertaken by the Fathers of the Christian church, found its completion. As son of a heathen father and a Christian mother, Augustine brought to the task not only his extraordinary gifts of mind and spirit but, above all, a passionate urge to overcome a set of contradictions in which he himself was directly involved. On his mother's side, Augustine was the immediate heir of Latin Christianity with all of the characteristic, almost puritanical austerity that arose from its fusion of Old Testament and Roman traits: moral seriousness, practical energy, devotion to ecclesiastical order and discipline, sober and rational observation of the commands and ordinances of God. What is new with him is the search of a passionate soul for really convincing truth, real belief, a search that leads to a historic intellectual encounter between this Latin Christianity and the spirit of the Greek East as embodied in the philosophy and theology of Neoplatonism and the New Testament.

Augustine's widely varied work in the form of philosophical dialogues, Bible commentaries, sermons, letters, controversial theological writings, and historical and autobiographical observations groups itself primarily around three main ideas. Augustine for the first time gave the emerging Western civilization a coherent world picture of its own. Weaving together Christian religion and Greek philosophy, incorporating and subordinating thought to belief, he equated the Christian conception of the things of this world as the realization of the thoughts of God with the Platonic conception of worldly things as the realization of eternal figures of being or ideas. Thus he united the two elements, the world as God's creation and the world as cosmos, the Biblical emphasis on the person and the Greek emphasis on the world, in a certain equilibrium—albeit a conditional one that was destined to break down again in the course of roughly a thousand years of passionate discussion.

The form in which this intellectual reconciliation was achieved was that of an advance from the god of Greek philosophy to the God of the Bible. In Neoplatonism, Augustine found for the first time a way of conceiving God that was appropriate to God's unlimited and all-embracing character—no longer as any kind of substance but, beyond all natural and material analogies, as spirit. But with Augustine this conception of God as spirit does not remain at the level of thought and sense impressions. Augustine seeks God not with the intellect alone but with all the forces of his mind and soul, with an inner need of the heart. Philosophy may provide an intellectual clarification of his original materialistic conceptions and doubts, but it affords no final satisfaction. His spirit forces its way upward in a passionate movement toward God himself, in an enthusiastic surrender to Him, in a hanging upon Him in belief, in hope, and in love that is altogether beyond philosophy.

It is thus that Augustine breaks through the hitherto impassable portals of the New Testament to penetrate and immerse himself more and more deeply in its contents. What he arrived at was no mere intellectual association, as for example in his identification of the Platonic ideas with the idea of God. Rather it was a passionate surrender that illuminated the whole of his remaining life and enabled him to bring about the fusion of these fundamentally disparate elements.

Hand in hand with this achievement goes Augustine's resumption of the Pauline teaching concerning the original sin of man and his total dependence on God's grace. This teaching is now extended into the doctrine of the unconditional predestination of man, the total predetermination by God of his fate in regard to salvation. In his insistence upon the total efficacy and complete freedom of God's grace, Augustine brought clearly to expression the idea that what counts in the religious domain is always primarily God and not man, and that even our belief is rightly understood only as something accomplished through God's grace. In making grace the central concept of Western theology, Augustine brought it into a decisive contradiction with Eastern Orthodox theology.

This separation was further deepened by the second of Augustine's main achievements, the historical philosophy presented in the *City of God*. In this great work Augustine developed his world picture in the Biblical sense of a historical process, coordinated with God's plan of salvation as symbolically manifested in the six days of creation. This last great apologia of the Church against heathendom projects the basic antinomy between arrogance and humility from the domain of the individual life to the course of universal history. Conceiving these two attitudes as characteristic of the *civitas terrena* and the *civitas dei*, respectively, Augustine follows the parallel development of the two domains from their origin in Adam's fall down to the collapse of Rome.

In taking the Roman church as the earthly counterpart of this heathen Roman Empire and thus as the incorporation and representative of the *civitas dei,* Augustine completely bypasses the myth of Byzantium as the "new, Christian Rome." Once again, he gives to the development of the Latin church of the West a decisive turn that leads it further and further away from the imperial Byzantine church and, ultimately, toward the schism between Rome and Byzantium.

Finally, Augustine developed the Biblical concern with man into a vast inquiry into the human personality. In a flood of philosophical dialogues and treatises, sermons and theological commentaries, letters and apologetic pamphlets, as well as in his autobiography and his world history, Augustine examined the problem of human individuality, such questions as the essence of the soul, the conscience, the conflict between insight and will, freedom of the will. Augustine stands at the end of the period of antiquity like a towering colossus on whom converge all the various lines of development of Judaism and Christianity, Greek and Roman civilization. They come together in his hands and then separate again in new divergences that persist in their basic lines down to our own day.

THE MEDIEVAL WORLD

It was during Augustine's lifetime (A.D. 354–430) that the world of the Biblical–Graeco-Roman civilization reached its end. As with the disintegration of the Egyptian-Mesopotamian civilization some thousand years earlier, its collapse was essentially the result of internal factors. Three of the four spiritual forces that had animated it—Judaism, Greek and Roman civilizations—had exhausted themselves. Christianity alone was in full ascent, and it was only beginning to exert an influence in secular affairs. From its very origins, in fact, this new movement had stood in a relationship of fundamental tension toward the whole of secular civilization, a tension that found its clearest expression precisely in

Augustine's *City of God*. The transformation of Christianity from a spiritual force that stood aloof from the world into a force that would gradually take over and penetrate the secular order represented not so much the end of antiquity as the beginning of a new era.

The collapse of the cultural forces of the classical civilization was undoubtedly supplemented by other factors, among them the insecurity of the central power, the weakness of administrative coordination, the differences between the Roman and the Greek-Oriental parts of the empire, the exhaustion of important sources of raw materials, the outflow of precious metals to pay for luxury imports. These varied sources of weakness interacted upon and reinforced each other because of the lack of any central authority capable of grasping and mastering them over the long term.

It was Constantine the Great, at the beginning of the fourth century A.D., who first managed to oppose an effective barrier to this process of internal disintegration. Again, however, the form of dominion that Constantine established represents not so much a last derivative of the ancient world as the beginning of a new age. Its essential feature was the consolidation of the central power in a quasi-divine supreme rulership in whose hands were concentrated all the threads of the thoroughly reorganized judicial, administrative, economic, and military systems. The decisive point, however, was the durable foundation that Constantine gave this new structure by raising Christianity to the position of a state religion and thus lending to his creation the support of the one spiritual force that was still alive.

Even this basic measure of internal consolidation did not suffice to preserve the unity of the empire, especially since Constantine reopened the gulf between its Roman and Greek-Oriental sections by moving the capital from Rome to Constantinople. The Roman, Western half of the empire broke down within less than two centuries, and large parts of the Eastern section yielded not long afterward to the advancing power of Islam. Nevertheless, the center of Constantine's creation, the Eastern Roman Empire grouped around the almost impregnable capital of Constantinople, managed to maintain itself throughout the whole course of the Middle Ages for a total of almost 1,200 years.

A second main factor that hastened the dissolution of the ancient and the formation of the medieval world was a change in the direction of the great barbarian invasions that had repeatedly stormed across the ancient world from the great Eurasian steppe to the north. During the last two centuries B.C. a succession of Indo-Germanic peoples had been moving from west to east to overflow the Mediterranean basin, the ancient Near East, India, and West Turkestan. A reversal occurred about the beginning of our era as swarms of Turkic, Mongolian, and Tungusic peoples began to flow from east to west in a contrary movement that lasted over a period of 1,500 years. While the pressure of the first Hunnic Empire was confined to China, India, and Iran, the advance of the second Hunnic Empire in the fourth century A.D. affected the new Christian Roman Empire along its entire northern front, partly by the agency of the Germanic tribes that were being driven before it and partly by that of the Hunnic hordes themselves. In the course of the following centuries the Huns were followed by the Avars, Bulgars, Hungarians, Rumanians, and Mongolians in the great plains and by the Turks and Mongolians in the east.

Interacting with these great Eurasian migrations was the advance of the Arabs from the south, as they stormed out of the Arabian peninsula in the new-found unity crystallized by Mohammed's proclamation of Islam early in the seventh century. Rapidly overrunning the enormous area extending from Spain in the west through the whole of North Africa and the Near East as far as Turkestan and India, they more or less completed the encircling movement begun by the incursions of the northern, Eurasian peoples. With the latter, the Islamic world formed a kind of barrier that separated the remains of the Roman Empire from the High Civilizations of India and China. By attracting and absorbing the impact of the Turkic and Mongolian peoples, it also formed a kind of defensive rampart behind which the medieval realms of the West could develop.

It was in this way that the internal disintegration of the ancient world, in conjunction with the external pressure of the Eurasian peoples on one side and the Arabs on the other, led to the tripartite division that constitutes the world of the Western Middle Ages. The West itself encompasses the Western half of the Roman Empire, overflowed by and divided up among the Germanic tribes, together with the Germanic-Slavic areas in central and northern Europe that are gradually brought within its orbit. The Byzantine realm comprises the Balkan peninsula and Asia Minor. The Islamic world basically includes (in addition to Iran) Syria, Egypt, North Africa, and large parts of Spain. Spiritually as well as territorially, all three of these domains shared in the heritage of the ancient world. The historical significance of the medieval period lies in the different ways in which these three civilizations developed their mutual inheritance.

Seen as a whole, the Middle Ages are a time of pause and even regression after the great forward movement of the Biblical–Graeco-Roman world. The flood of creative forces ebbs away. Further development, where it occurs at all, is quite limited; in most fields there is a more or less far-reaching collapse. The only major exception is found in the domain of religion. Here, the breakthrough to monotheism and the defeat of the mythical polytheistic religions is consolidated and extended through the spread of Christianity to the heathen Germanic and Slavic peoples in central and eastern Europe. The advent of Mohammed—the only religious personality of world-historical significance to emerge during this period—initiated a similar process affecting the peoples of Arabia, Iran, northwest India, and parts of Africa.

This consolidation and extension of Christianity and Islam in their respective territories involved an unprecedented process of cultural penetration, one in which the entire fabric of society came to be permeated as never before with religious feelings and concepts. Having placed the individual in an immediate, personal relationship to God, Judaism, Christianity, and Islam all claimed to determine his life in a measure and with a sternness unknown to the polytheistic religions.

But this extension of religion throughout the whole life of the peoples created an unavoidable tension between religious presuppositions and commands on the one side and the practical requirements of everyday reality on the other. This underlying tension between religion and the world was especially acute in Christianity, whose original radical independence from the world yielded only gradually to a progressive adaptation. Christianity's relationship to the world, in fact, was destined to remain essentially one of tension, a tension that could be and was bridged over in practice but which nevertheless remained irresolvable in principle—and had to remain so if its essence and unique source of strength were not to be surrendered. As already suggested, however, this tension was far stronger in the West than in Byzantium, a fact that held decisive significance for the inward development of the two branches of Christianity as well as their ultimate fate.

The situation in Islam was quite different. Mohammed was not only a prophet but a statesman as well. Religion for him was not something that stood in fundamental contradiction to the necessities of the world; on the contrary, it was a power that found its aim precisely in the political dominion and religious transformation of the world. The opposition between religion and the world that lay at the root of Christianity did not exist for Islam—or, at any rate, it was not an essential opposition but merely a practical one, a lack of practical concordance between religion and reality such as one might find in the misuse of religion by the political leadership. Islam, like Judaism, was primarily a religion of law. Not the relation of the soul to God, but the exact regulation of life stood in the foreground of its concern.

Both in Islam and in the West, the eclipse of the Graeco-Roman cities after almost a thousand years of hegemony over the Mediterranean basin led to a return to the political form of personal monarchy, the typical polity of the agricultural stage of human development. As the northern Germans and Slavs completed the destruction of the disintegrating Western Empire, they erected their own dominion on its ruins in a form that was to persist without substantial change down to the fall of the major historic dynasties in the first decades of the twentieth century.

But the personal rule established by the European monarchs differed in important respects from that of the Oriental kings, emperors, and caliphs. They, too, felt themselves to be ruling "by the grace of God," but they were very far from possessing unlimited power. Above them stood the living God of the Bible; and God's will, not theirs, was decisive. Over them, moreover, stood the law, whose requirements were as binding on them as on the least of their subjects. Their task was simply to preserve and implement the good old law which had come down from remote times. When they neglected or transgressed against this highest duty, they theoretically destroyed their own right of rulership. Their subjects then won a valid right of resistance against them.

Not less significant than these theoretical limitations on the European rulers was their practical limitation by the feudal system. The nominal rulers of Europe were by no means the sovereign masters of their realms. They could not freely dispose of their territories or appoint and discharge their representatives. They themselves were simply the highest representatives of an ambitious class of territorial magnates who had divided up the European lands among themselves. As the highest rank in this class of magnates, the rulers were doubly bound: ideally by the conception of the feudal system as a system of reciprocal bonds and relationships of good faith; materially by the difficulties of getting past their immediate feudatories to seek support from the feudatories of the latter.

Together, the institution of rulership and the feudal system determined the political structure of medieval Europe. The cities occupied a subordinate position. They, too, experienced a significant advance and extension through the founding of numerous new cities, especially in connection with the process of colonization in the East. But the medieval cities, unlike their ancient counterparts, were not independent political communities but economic centers that remained more or less dependent on the ruling territorial powers. Nevertheless, they were able to develop within their walls a powerful, sober, but far-seeing spirit of citizenship and, so long as the organization of Europe by the rising territorial states remained incomplete, to win important power positions in the unpre-empted areas of the Mediterranean, in the frontier regions between France and Germany, and in the Baltic. But this position was lost with the growing strength of the territorial powers. Only the Italian city-republics were able to maintain their independence until well into modern times.

The medieval world with its numerous spiritual and political forces was held together primarily by the Church and, in a considerably less degree, by the institutions of the Holy Roman Empire. The church spanned the whole of Christendom with its archbishoprics, bishoprics, and parishes, with the cloisters, churches, and chapels that together constituted a giant network extending into the most remote corners of Europe. It developed the cycle of the year into an annual dramatic renewal of the Christian story. Over the earth stretched the vault of heaven, the seat of God and His angels. Deep within it lay the opposite pole of hell. Within this spiritual framework, the world formed a comprehensive hierarchical order with the Emperor as overlord and with sharply drawn distinctions between the various estates. Each had its own special tasks, each its special rights and duties.

Thus the Western civilization of the Middle Ages was able to fuse and weld together the multiplicity of converging and intercrossing traditions and forces that composed it into a whole of really astonishing coherence. As compared with the one-sidedness of both the Biblical and the Greek traditions, the various opposing tendencies seemed effectually joined together and brought into equilibrium. Spiritual and worldly authority, law and power, strength and intimate feeling stood side by side, supplementing and reciprocally limiting each other. In this comprehensive harmony ordained by God, nothing seemed to stand for itself alone, neither thought nor feeling, neither angel nor man, beast, plant, or inanimate thing. Everything possessed, in addition to its immediately given reality, a deep symbolic meaning. Everything was bound together with everything else and, in the last analysis, with the Creator of all these things. In the Western civilization of the Middle Ages, the old basic form of the High Civilizations, the universal world system that was bound together and balanced in all directions, found its last and most comprehensive realization in a form that had been clarified and rationalized by Biblical and Greek thought.

The Middle Ages reached its apogee between the eleventh and thirteenth centuries. From that point onward a new trend becomes apparent. The civilization that had been built up did not consolidate itself further but began to disintegrate again. The unity of the church was visibly shaken and only painfully reestablished in a series of great ecclesiastical councils. The papacy and the Empire suffered a diminution in authority and practical power and drifted away from each other. The weakening authority of the Empire diluted the sense of unity of the Christian West to the advantage of the emerging national states. The hierarchical formation of medieval society began to lose its strength under the influence of an expanding money and market economy. The reconciliation of faith and thought established by Augustine gave place to an increasingly sharp separation and opposition.

And yet this dissolution of medieval civilization in the fourteenth and fifteenth centuries was no downfall but a rise, no last spasm of expiring forces but the powerful surging of new ones. In the civilization of the Middle Ages three powerful advancing forces—the Christian religion with its message of salvation, the Graeco-Roman heritage with its tradition of rational thought, and the fresh forces of the northern peoples with their passionate way of feeling—had come into contact and reciprocally restrained and limited each other. The passion of Christian belief had been neutralized by its association with the balanced character of Greek philosophy, especially Plato and Aristotle; the revolutionary tendencies of Greek rationality had been similarly contained by the primacy of faith. The Christian and the northern striving for domination had mutually limited each other in the claims to authority of papacy and Empire. The whole artfully balanced structure had held down and restrained the innate passion of the northern peoples.

But the spirit that gave rise to these limitations ran counter to the basic tendency of the very forces that were being held in check. The essential dynamism of these forces contrasted sharply with the extremely static character of the medieval outlook. Wholly concentrated on authority and stability, the medieval mind had an almost involuntary tendency to recognize authorities of the most varied kinds and somehow or other accommodate them to each other. It thought entirely in static-hierarchical concepts in its view of the world as in its view of society. It was fundamentally inclined to uphold the old, the inherited, and to give it preeminence over the new.

Thus, while the Middle Ages undoubtedly achieved an astounding scope and balance, which are reflected in the greatness of its cultural achievements, the contradiction between its basically static attitude and the dynamism of the forces that flowed together in it was too deep for the latter to be really mastered or lastingly incorporated into its structure. They could only be dammed back for a couple of hundred years. As the bonds holding this civilization together began to weaken more and more in the course of the fourteenth and fifteenth centuries, the dam itself was strained and weakened to such an extent that at the end of the fifteenth century these long pent-up forces broke through in an overpowering stream.

3

The Breakthrough to
the Modern Era

THE SUDDEN breakthrough of the forces that had been building up in medieval civilization was of decisive importance not only for the fate of Western man but also, on a much broader scale, for the whole agricultural stage of human development. Since the very beginning of the agricultural stage almost 10,000 years before, its whole development had been characterized by an equilibrium between progressive tendencies and restraining and consolidating forces. The basic trend of the agricultural period—the impulse of men toward consolidation of their existence in a coherent world picture—had remained alive through all these millennia, and the progress of the advancing forces had been so comparatively limited that such a consolidation could in fact take place again and again. Thus, while the general cultural level had been significantly raised in the course of the agricultural period, this process had been so slow that the harmony between progress and consolidation was either maintained unbroken or could at least be continually re-established. It is this harmony and balance that were to be increasingly disrupted from the fifteenth century onward.

At the same time that Western civilization broke through from the Middle Ages to modern times, each of the three other main civilizations went through a comparable period of advance: the Islamic world under the Ottoman caliphs, India under the Mogul dynasty, China under the Manchus. Remarkable as they were in themselves, however, each of these advances in the non-Western world remained within the inherited religious-political-cultural framework of the agricultural period. Only Western civilization, with its unique synthesis of the revolutionary forces of Christianity, the Graeco-Roman cultural tradition, and the energies of the northern peoples, effected a radical break with the traditional framework of the agricultural period, thus raising itself to a completely new level of existence and ultimately dragging the other civilizations along after it. This truly epoch-making breakthrough expressed itself primarily in a flood of new forces in all the fields of human existence. Far from becoming exhausted after a few generations or centuries, moreover, this stream of new forces was unceasingly to renew itself as it constantly increased in volume and scope.

THE POST-MEDIEVAL OUTLOOK

This ever more tumultuous surge of advancing forces in Western civilization reflects a radical change in the outlook of the men who initiated it. Throughout the agricultural period this outlook had remained essentially the same in all of the different civilizations. Its root was the pre-eminence of the world over man, the incorporation of the individual into the prevailing world system. Now, suddenly, this relationship was abruptly reversed. To the man of the modern era, it was no longer the world that appeared decisive and controlling, but man himself. No longer did he see himself as simply a particle incorporated into the towering structure of the world, subordinated to its rhythms and laws, exposed to its unpredictable moods and blows of fate. Now, for the first time, he began to feel himself independent vis-à-vis the world,

not so much a member of it as rather its active midpoint. Filled
with the proud sense of this new independence, he divested himself one by one of the traditional limitations on his thoughts and
desires and dared to base himself simply and solely on the strength
of his own reason. As he learned to penetrate the world with the
strength of this reason, he laid aside his sense of dependence,
undertook a more and more active role in relation to the world,
intervened increasingly in its arrangements, and began freely to
transform it according to his own ideas.

With this basic change in man's attitude, the subjective traits
that had hitherto determined his point of view were equally transformed. Where hitherto he had been filled with an unconditional
trust in the authorities placed above him, this confidence was now
torn to shreds amid the growing conflict of diverse authorities.
Where he had been accustomed to build upon the traditional, the
constantly recurring, he now began to attach value to the new,
simply because it was new, and to set off in quest of what had
never been before. Where previously he had regarded equilibrium
and moderation as the highest virtues, he now strove for the extreme, recklessly following each new path to its furthest consequences. Where once he had anxiously noted the boundaries
surrounding him and even voluntarily traced boundaries for
himself, he now pressed boldly into the unknown where there
seemed to be no boundaries at all.

This basic transformation did not take place all at once. At first,
the new dynamic attitude that found its inspiration in the sovereign ego tended to assert itself only in principle. Its protagonists—
the great religious innovators in all camps, the great intellectual
pioneers from Descartes to Hegel, the great political architects of
the modern states—stood in a definitely ambivalent relationship
to the new world. They were revolutionaries and conservatives at
the same time. They tore down with one hand only to build up
all the more firmly with the other. Attempting to use the flood of
liberated forces for their own works, they believed that these same
forces could be bound and laid to rest by those works themselves.

Thus the development of the modern era takes the form not of a single, unified, and continuous movement but of a series of new beginnings, a succession of steps, each one of which was intended to bring its accomplishment to a conclusion and consolidate the results—but each of which was promptly superseded and thrust aside in its turn by the forces that had been set in motion. Finally, in the course of the nineteenth century, this series of attempted consolidations breaks off altogether. The completely new and radically dynamic character of modern civilization as a continuous forward surge, extending further and further beyond every frontier, finally establishes itself and is consciously recognized as its guiding principle.

SECULARIZATION

This radical transformation of the Western outlook developed initially in the critical sphere of religion. In itself Western culture, in conformity with the Biblical tradition and the general outlook of its peoples, was a definitely religious culture, and the turn toward the modern era did not in any sense imply a repudiation of this religious basis. In contrast to the visible weakening of religious impulses in the later Middle Ages, the modern era originated in a passionate renewal of these very impulses, one that found its most dramatic expression in the Reformation and Counter Reformation.

Unfortunately, however, this passionate surge of religious feeling did not lead to an integral renewal but was broken up by an embittered division of belief, with the result that its strength was gradually exhausted during the century and a half of the religious struggle in Europe. Yet even the gradual abatement of this religious conflict did not by any means betoken a departure from the religious basis as such. The Bible still remained the common foundation of Western civilization, for the masses as well as the educated; its basic doctrines remained the common preconceptions of Western thought and feeling. Without this influence, neither the development of the modern absolute state nor that of modern democracy, neither modern science nor the modern economy would have been conceivable.

What actually changed in the modern era was not the religious basis as such but rather the function of religion within the whole cultural structure. Up to this time, religion had everywhere been regarded as pre-eminently a public affair. Even where a religion was not directly identified with the state and a number of religions coexisted within the same state, membership in a religion had a determining influence on its practitioners' outlook and on their position in public life. The decisive change that occurred as Western civilization entered the modern era was that while the various religions continued to maintain their purely religious claims, they lost their public character. The states separated themselves from the churches, confessions ceased to be matters of public concern and became the private affairs of the individual believers.

In thus losing its public character, religion at the same time lost its predominant influence in other fields. This weakening in the hitherto all-pervasive influence of religion cleared the way for the unimpeded development of political thought and organization, of philosophy and science. The same shift from an objective or public to a subjective or personal point of view provided the revolutionary impulse in each of these separate fields.

THE MODERN STATE AND THE PRIVATE SPHERE

The second decisive development in the breakthrough to the modern era was the creation of the modern state. Both of the two main state forms that had existed up to this time, the territorial state and the city-state, had in their different ways been established on a personal far more than on an institutional basis. The territorial states depended on the purely personal rule of their supreme ruler and on his personal relationship to the leading class of great landowning families. The city-states rested on the narrow basis of the personal relationships within the citizenry, in which the limited development of the institutional apparatus was compensated by the unique intensity of a political life in which every internal conflict tended to develop with merciless sharpness.

A remarkable feature of the development of the modern institutional state was that to a certain extent it took place in defiance of all natural historical logic. According to such logic one would have expected a repetition of the Greek experience, in which the extreme personal form of rulership, that of the territorial prince, was set aside by the nobility and this in turn was supplanted by the cities. Instead of this, it was precisely the territorial rulers who managed to free their power from the strict limitations imposed by medieval conditions and to increase it to a height of absolutism hardly less than that of the Oriental despots.

A second remarkable feature of this process was that the territorial princes carried out this consolidation of their purely personal rule in direct opposition to the feudal powers, and with means dependent not on personal but precisely on institutional relationships. The great ruler figures and ministers who built up the modern state replaced the feudal relationships of the Middle Ages by a modern, rationalized, institutional state apparatus with its professionally schooled civil service, its bureaucratically regulated order of business, its economic and statistical methods. Above all, they replaced the feudal levies or the scarcely more reliable mercenary armies with permanent military instruments in the form of standing armies and navies.

But in thus establishing the unlimited personal rule of the prince through the consolidation of an entirely impersonal instrument of power, they unavoidably gave to this impersonal and institutional power apparatus a life and a weight of its own that made it, far more than the prince, the real bearer of rule. The state, which the absolute princes regarded as their completely free possession, developed under their hands into an independent power configuration with its own objective interests and goals, its own *raison d'état*. In view of this tendency toward independence on the part of their own creations, there was nothing left for the rulers as individuals except to incorporate themselves into the latter as the first servants of their states—or, alternatively, to content themselves with a mere representational role as a sort of honorary presiding officer.

A third critical feature of this process by which the feudal state was transformed into the modern state was the opposition between continental states on one side and maritime states on the other, or between absolute and constitutional states. The continental states—Spain, France, Austria, Prussia—were exposed to the full pressure of the universal struggle for power that prevailed within the European community of states as it formed itself out of medieval Christendom. Their policy and development were governed by the complete primacy of external politics. All their efforts were directed toward maintaining themselves in this merciless struggle. In all of them, and especially in states like France and Prussia, which found themselves hemmed in by a whole group of powerful neighbors, this continuous pressure from outside accelerated the tendency toward consolidation of power. Sharp concentration of political authority in the hands of the monarch, concentration of the state resources on the development of military strength, emphasis on the state idea, on the unconditional supremacy of the public interest, characterized them all.

In this sharp emphasis on state interests, the absolute state was merely reasserting that unconditional pre-eminence of the community over its members that had been traditional since the primeval horde. The only difference was that this attitude, in conformity with what we have described as the general tendency of the modern era, was now being pushed to its extreme consequences. The state, according to the generally accepted view, was the whole that was there before its parts and remained entirely superior to them. The state ruled over its subjects absolutely, at least in theory and often enough in practice. It assigned them their place in its development and intervened in their existence in the most varied ways. What was modern about it was not its basic attitude, but simply its new institutional apparatus and its one-sided orientation toward the struggle for power, as we see it, for instance, in Machiavelli. These modern traits did not diminish but only accentuated the state's dominant character.

The maritime states, first England and the Netherlands and later the English overseas colonies, differed from the continental states in that they were to a large degree withdrawn from the immediate pressure of the European state system and its power struggle of all against all. With the external pressure so much reduced, the ruling princes could not put through the consolidation of their power in anything like the same measure. The stadholders of the House of Orange had to struggle again and again with the opposition of the States-General. In England a similar conflict led first to the execution of Charles I and thereafter, in the revolution of 1688, to the establishment of the full-fledged constitutional state.

The emergence of the constitutional state represented much more than simply the establishment of a maritime counterpart to the absolute state. It represented a fundamental turning point in the whole development of the state, one whose historical meaning is seldom sufficiently recognized. Unlike the absolute state, the constitutional state was something more than just the traditional state equipped with modern means and aims. It was, from the ground up, a completely new creation. It was the political expression of what we have described as the basic tendency of the modern era, the devaluation of the objective world in favor of the claims of the subjective ego. In radical contrast to the absolute state, it was built up on the theory expounded by Hobbes and Locke in the seventeenth century that the main thing was *not* the state or the community but the individuals in it. No longer is it a case of the state being there and molding the individuals to its needs. It was rather the individuals who, having joined together to constitute a society, created the state as their instrument and determined its goals and limits.

According to this novel conception, the state was nothing else and nothing more than a service organ of society, an organization that society had voluntarily set up to maintain order internally and defense externally. In sharp contrast to the traditional concept of the state, which was unequivocally based on the duties of the individual to the community, the theory of the constitutional state was based not on the individual's duties but on his rights. Where the absolute state gave to the state itself the absolute position, the constitutional state gave this position to society—which means, in the last analysis, to the individual.

This placing of society in an absolute position in relation to the state gave to the individual a freedom of attitude that he had never before known under any form of rule. In all previous political communities, not excluding the Roman, the individual in the last analysis had stood defenseless under the community's pressure. The community determined him completely, not only in the fulfillment of his communal duties but also, in greater or less degree, in his purely personal affairs. Insofar as the individual was able to win for himself a personal sphere in relation to the community, this was granted him only on a conditional and revocable basis. But now, in the constitutional state, the individual for the first time found himself essentially withdrawn from the pressure of his community in virtue of the fact that he himself, rather than the state, had been placed at the center of the political constellation.

At the same time, this new freedom in relation to the state carried with it an ambiguity of the deepest significance. As the individual became free of the state, there opened before him the possibility of two alternative and directly opposite attitudes toward it. On one side, the citizen of the constitutional state, like his predecessors in the horde, the village community, the ancient and medieval city-state, was a participant in the community, a citizen. As such he had a part in and an influence upon the public tasks and decisions of the state. Like the citizens of the ancient city-states, he could make devotion to public affairs the real content of his life. From this standpoint, the establishment of the constitutional state led logically and directly to modern democracy.

On the other side, he was also a private individual, something that had been true only in a very precarious way if at all under all previous forms of rule. Hitherto no political form had permitted a clear-cut division between public and private affairs. Now, with the turn from the state to the individual, such a division became entirely possible. Seen from the standpoint of the state, public affairs could never be clearly delimited; but they could be so delimited from the individual's standpoint. Public affairs were simply those tasks that he and his fellow citizens had expressly classified as such in entrusting their regulation and observation to the state. Everything else, everything that had not been expressly turned over to the state by popular decision, was *ipso facto* declared as private. In other words, it was declared to be something which fundamentally did not concern the community, about which the latter had nothing to say in principle, and in which the individual reserved the right not merely to a voice but to complete freedom of operation according to his unrestricted judgment or even caprice.

With this fundamental separation between the state and society, between the individual as a citizen and the individual as a private person, we reach the end result of the long and complicated process by which the modern state was developed and consolidated. Measured against the limitation of the individual by his community that prevailed under all earlier state forms, the establishment of the private sphere as an area withdrawn in principle from the interference of the community represented a really fundamental turning point in the political and even in the general cultural development of mankind. If we are no longer conscious of its historical significance today, it is only because we have grown so accustomed to it in the course of the past century that it now seems to us obvious and natural.

Yet this change opened up new problems of the most fundamental character, which up to the present time have found no adequate clarification, let alone solution. The passage of time has made it increasingly clear that this modern, basic separation between the public and the private spheres represents a no less one-sided solution than the previous pre-eminence of the public over the private. Such a separation is not of the kind that can be established once and for all. The line between the things that require regulation by the community and those that can and must be left to private initiative has been continually moving back and forth in the course of the last centuries, at first in the direction of a growing limitation of the public sphere but, within the last hundred years, primarily in the direction of its widening again. But to establish this relationship and redefine it over and over again in a really just fashion would require a genuine equilibrium between the two basic points of view, those of public and private interest, rather than a one-sided pre-eminence of the private over the public such as still tends to prevail at the present time.

SCIENCE AND TECHNOLOGY

The third basic element in the breakthrough of Western civilization to the modern age was that of modern science and technology. Modern science, in its basic impulses, was a product of modern philosophy. Scientific investigators like Copernicus, Giordano Bruno, and Galileo found it necessary to come to terms with the philosophical basis of traditional science, especially the overpowering authority of Aristotle, in order to open a path for their own researches. In turn, philosophers like Descartes, Pascal, and Leibniz prepared the ground for modern science, developed its basic presuppositions and methods, its mathematical aids. As a result of these efforts, science, like philosophy, went through the characteristically modern shift from the world to the self, from passive observation to active investigation.

But here their ways separated. While philosophy reached a stalemate in its constantly renewed endeavor to arrive at a lasting solution of the problems opened up by this shift in viewpoints, modern science was able to establish a dependable basis for itself. This it could do because it was more and more consciously freeing itself from philosophy's absolute quest for truth and limiting itself to a purely hypothetical, provisional quest for truth, one that enabled and indeed compelled it to regard each scientific insight simply as one step in an endless process, as an insight which was only there in order to be superseded by other, deeper, and better founded insights.

Modern science was in a position to establish and confirm these hypothetical, provisional insights in a quite different manner than was available to philosophy. By replacing the emphasis on observation that had characterized all previous science with the use of experiments, it acquired a revolutionary methodological tool with which to attack the objects of its investigation. Above all, its results were freed from the subjectivity of the individual researcher, since the same experiment was bound to produce the same results when repeated by any other investigator.

To these two foundations of modern science—hypothetical theory and its corollary, the experiment either confirming or disproving it—was added a third in modern mathematics. Mathematics had by this time freed itself from the limitations and inflexibility of Greek mathematical thought and was being elaborated into an increasingly comprehensive and highly developed intellectual system. The astonishing feature of this system was not only that it could be made consistent in itself, but that an intellectual system based on this inner consistency could actually provide the key to the external structure of nature. Quite unexpectedly, nature revealed itself to be built up on the basis of mathematically formulatable relationships and, even more remarkable, quite simple mathematical relationships. Nothing contributed so much to the success and self-confidence of the modern natural sciences as the fact that the basic relationships in nature could be reduced to the simplest possible mathematical formulas, from Galileo's laws of gravity through Kepler's equations for the planetary orbits and Newton's equations for motion and universal gravitation to Einstein's formula for the relationship between energy and mass.

This completely new association of hypothetical theory, practical experiment, and mathematical interpretation set modern natural science on a road that led beyond mere brilliant individual achievement. The experimentally confirmed and mathematically formulated results of natural science acquired an objective validity that permitted the fusion of individual accomplishments into a single, consolidated process. As a collective research process, modern science not only came to be depersonalized and institutionalized to a high degree; it was increasingly converted from a series of sporadic and unorganized efforts into an ever more planned and rationalized process, from individual achievements into a cumulative chain-reaction system. As the breakthrough to the modern era progressed, modern science emerged more and more clearly as the most purely developed manifestation of modern civilization in its character as an unceasing process.

Of decisive importance to this development was the fact that modern science found in modern mathematics a unique instrument of synthesis as well as analysis. By reducing the sensuous qualities of things to mathematical relationships, phenomena of the most varied qualitative characteristics could be brought into quantitative relationship with one another. Not everything could be quantified in this way, and not everything that was quantified could be reduced "to the same common denominator." Nevertheless, modern science was able to achieve, if not a total synthesis of its knowledge, at least comprehensive partial syntheses: Newton's mechanics, the laws of thermodynamics, modern atomic physics, Einstein's theory of relativity. Because of this unique association of analysis and synthesis, modern natural science was in a position not only to exemplify in the clearest and most consistent way the basic peculiarity of modern culture—its development as a continuing process—but also to avoid to a large extent the concomitant dangers of specialization, fragmentation, and loss of the over-all view. That it failed to avoid them completely will be evident from a later chapter. However, the development of modern natural science became the basic factor in the development of modern technology and, as a final consequence, of modern industrial civilization.

THE INDUSTRIAL REVOLUTION

The breakthrough to the modern era that began with the secularization of Western culture and continued with the development of the modern state and its private society was completed in the industrial revolution. The process of secularization created the ideological framework for this development by substituting for the medieval economic outlook, with its emphasis on such non-economic considerations as the just price and the prohibition of interest, a new economic outlook entirely oriented toward the market economy. The development of the modern state created the political and legal framework by establishing the private sphere as an area whose autonomous and legally protected status made possible the weaving together of economic, technical, and scientific developments into the entirely new process of industrialization. It was certainly no accident that this process began in England, the country that had been first to develop the framework of the constitutional state and had done so in the most consistent manner.

For the industrial revolution in its origins was in no sense a public process, but a completely private one. Its roots were located entirely in the private sphere, which it transformed by completely private, purely economic processes. Above all, it occurred without any conscious intention on the part of its protagonists. It was a wholly unforeseen, unintended, unplanned development. Daring and enterprising individuals, exclusively concerned with the furthering of their private economic advantage, took hold of the new possibilities and brought them into being. Their operations, at first purely individual and wholly uncoordinated, immediately began to weave themselves into a general economic-technical-scientific process that very rapidly acquired a life of its own.

What was completely new in the industrial revolution was its overwhelming drive, its "punch." The agricultural revolution, as we have seen, had also brought about a complete transformation in the conditions of its own time. But this earlier transformation had nevertheless remained a limited process. Cultivation and animal husbandry, by their very nature, were capable of only a narrowly limited development. In the further course of the agricultural era, the High Civilizations had brought about important advances in handicrafts and long-distance trade. But the resultant progress did not transcend the limits traced by the general level of the agricultural period.

In the earlier course of the modern era, however, this general level had already been raised to such an extent that the political structure, the legal security, the economic and financial means, and the transport facilities required for the advance to industrial production were already available. At the same time, the transition to industrial production created an economic form which, in contrast to agriculture and animal husbandry, handicrafts and trade, was absolutely unlimited in its capacity for expansion. Once set in motion, the industrial revolution developed under the hands of its originators from a forward step that had still been limited in time and substance into an absolutely unlimited process of transformation. It converted itself into an unending process of constantly increasing depth, range, power, and rapidity.

The result of this broadening of the industrial revolution from a one-time transformation of the methods of production into a continuously expanding process of transformation was a parallel transformation of the bases of human existence—not merely from one level to a higher level, but from one form of existence, the essentially static one of the agricultural era, to a completely different one, the essentially dynamic one of the new industrial period. This change had originated in the methods of production but was in no sense limited to them. Starting with textiles and iron products, the new industrial techniques increasingly exerted their influence on the other branches of handicraft production. Concurrently, due to the cheapness and abundance of its products, industrialization began to revolutionize the whole popular way of life in such matters as clothing and food, housing and public health, communications and news dissemination.

As a function of these material transformations, the industrial revolution called into existence not only a completely new way of life but a new human type adapted to it. By radically transforming the whole cultural structure through the methods of production, it came to represent nothing less than the basic movement, the primary motive force of the whole development of Western civilization; and from the West it increasingly extended its influence to the other civilizations as well. Mankind's way of life was transformed from an "existence" into an unending "process."

This extension of the industrial revolution from a partial to a universal cultural development, from a limited to an unlimited process, raised completely new problems of guidance and direction. Hitherto the general cultural level had been so low and the cultural structure so simple that the processes of development could be either planned from above or, if not planned, at least controlled. Cultural developments had been matters of public concern, in the sense that as public affairs they were subject to regulation from above. However defective, self-interested, and blind such regulation had often been in practice, the principle of regulation, the principle that matters of public concern could not simply be left to themselves, had been accepted as obvious from the primitive horde right down to the modern state.

The modern constitutional state, however, had now created in the private sphere an area that had not, in principle, seemed to require such regulation. There had been a tacit assumption that developments in the private sphere would remain so limited in scope that they would not significantly affect the public interest. In practice, the industrial revolution completely overthrew this assumption. Through the sudden tremendous intensification of economic and hence of social relationships, these mass processes acquired a force that not only transformed developments in the private sphere in the most radical way but extended their influence from the private into the public sphere and decisively affected public affairs as well.

In this sense the industrial revolution was indeed a revolution, that is, an overthrow of the whole cultural structure. But because it was a private and not a public revolution, it was also a wholly unintended, totally unplanned, and even largely unconscious one. The entrepreneurs who carried it through did not have the slightest intention of bringing about a public overturn by their private activities. They therefore continued to regard these private undertakings as entirely private affairs, to be regulated solely by the economic mechanisms of the market economy. What this meant was that cultural processes, which from the standpoint of their results were of a public nature and therefore demanded public regulation, were left essentially unregulated.

Thus the industrial revolution emerged as a completely new type of development not only in its extent but also in the way it was steered and managed. While its power increased by leaps and bounds and increasingly transformed all fields of human existence, the gigantic forces it had unloosed continued to be left essentially to themselves. As a result, this unique process of development was carried out under conditions of harshness and sacrifice that could have been avoided had it taken place in even a half-planned fashion. The masses of the new industrial proletariat were transplanted out of the meager conditions of their rural existence into new and artificial environments that at first were very much harder. Only gradually did the idea develop that these conditions were a matter of public concern which did require public regulation.

While the rigors to which the working masses were exposed did not indefinitely escape public attention, another and deeper consequence of the industrial revolution remained almost entirely unperceived. From its very beginning this movement had carried within itself an essential contradiction. It was charged with an overwhelming power unlike anything previously known in man's experience; yet this overwhelming and constantly increasing power was not controlled or directed according to any general plan or intellectual concept. While some of the resultant problems, such as the exploitation of the new industrial proletariat, were essentially transitional and capable of being remedied, others were of a more basic and continuing nature because they developed out of the very structure of the new industrial societies.

In these societies men were abruptly dissociated from their traditional activities as peasants, artisans, and craftsmen and herded together in masses in the slums and factories of the new industrial centers. The old, simple, understandable relationships between men and their livelihoods, between men and their neighbors, were replaced by complex impersonal relationships. The increasing specialization of work tied people more and more to their place in the system and made them dependent upon vast economic processes that were completely beyond their control and even their understanding. An economic crisis in some distant continent or the development of a new process of production could throw men out of work without their even knowing why.

These new societies were wholly artificial constructions, developed strictly in accordance with industrial criteria. As compared, for example, with the Greek city-states, they were totally lacking in form and coherence. The individual felt lost in them. They cut him off from nature, yet failed to afford him the possibility of building a really independent existence for himself. Increasingly men found themselves placed in the midst of relationships that at bottom were entirely incomprehensible to them. In freeing himself from the bondage of nature, man was thus becoming more and more "alienated" from his natural inheritance and began to find himself bound anew in circumstances that threatened to prove far more intolerable than the old ones.

THE THEORY OF ALIENATION

The breakthrough of Western civilization to the modern era, then, was the product of a constantly growing stream of energies that not only surpassed all earlier experience but continued to increase from year to year. It was small wonder that these changes soon began to exert an influence in the realm of the intellect. The basic tendencies of the agricultural period, as we have seen, had been directed toward the achievement of a harmony and balance that were made attainable in practice by the inherent limitations of the existing material, social, and spiritual relationships. Now, in consequence of the continuous intensification of dynamic forces in every field, the cultural tendencies that had thus far been held in equilibrium began to define themselves more sharply, to differentiate themselves, and to come into conflict with each other. We have seen this happening in the intellectual field in the growing division between faith and knowledge; in the political realm, in the distinction between the citizen and the private individual; in the economic and social fields, in the incipient opposition between bourgeoisie and proletariat.

At first these divisions were obscured by the overwhelming sense of progress that filled the earlier centuries of the modern era and stamped the eighteenth century in particular as the period of Enlightenment. Insofar as the Enlightenment recognized such conflicts at all, it viewed them as survivals of earlier, "unreasonable" conditions that would be overcome within a foreseeable time by the victorious force of reason. It was only when this naïvely optimistic expectation had proved completely groundless, when Western culture instead of progressing along the road to more and more enlightenment found itself plunged in a series of fundamental internal conflicts, that such contradictions came to be recognized as a real problem deserving of serious attention.

The attempt at a basic confrontation with the problems raised by the breakthrough into modern times began in the period of the great revolutions of the late eighteenth century and continued through most of the nineteenth century until, toward the end of that period, it was abandoned amid a new wave of optimism. It was the work of a handful of towering thinkers who combined an extraordinary sense of reality, a highly developed sensitivity to the real processes concealed beneath the appearance of ever-broadening progress, and an equally unique gift of intellectual penetration and formulation. Among them, Hegel and Marx particularly stand out not only because of their nearness to the events of their time but because of the comprehensive framework in which they attempted to place them.

Hegel and Marx were actually the first to conceive the evolution of mankind—from its beginnings in the formation of the human species and the primitive horde down to the political and industrial transformations of their own time—as a single process of development. Both of them, moreover, were alike in taking an essentially positive view of this process, in which they saw a predominantly upward development toward reason and freedom. This was true despite the fact that they had abandoned the naïve spirit of the Enlightenment and insisted that such a development could occur only through the overcoming of a series of deep-rooted contradictions. Yet despite their far-reaching parallelism, their deep and comprehensive analyses of man's development are different from the ground up. The differences begin with their diametrically opposed conceptions of man himself.

Man, for Hegel, is not just something given. He is, to begin with, an animal. To become a man, he must first carry out a fundamental act of self-conquest in order to overcome the animal in himself, free himself from mere existence as a part of nature, and establish himself as a moral and intellectual individual. "Man," Hegel wrote in the 1820's in *The Philosophy of World History*, "must make himself into what he is to be; he himself must achieve everything for himself, precisely because he is mind; he must get rid of the natural."

For Marx, on the other hand, the nature of man is established not by his break with nature but precisely by his fulfillment of nature. Man, for Marx, does not *become* man; he has *been* man from the very beginning, precisely through his original naturalness, in the immediate unity and fullness and the unbroken development of his natural tendencies and drives. *"Man* is an immediate *natural being*," Marx wrote in the "Paris manuscripts" of 1844. Man is "the real, bodily *man* who stands on the firm and well-based earth, exhaling and inhaling all natural forces."

This basic difference in the conception of man leads Hegel and Marx to equally different interpretations of his development. For Hegel, the development of man as a morally and intellectually free personality is crystallized in the state, the organic totality of a people, and his development to freedom proceeds through a succession of leading states in which one replaces the other. For Marx, on the other hand, the development of mankind takes place not in the state but in society, the original and natural frame of man's existence and the arena of the struggle between classes that represents the real content and motive force of history. The development of man, in Marx's eyes, proceeds not from state to state but from class to class. The political development of mankind is merely a distorted superstructure on top of the real socio-economic development.

Thus Hegel and Marx see the development of mankind as coming to its completion in fundamentally different circumstances. For Hegel, the history of man's development, being political history, ends in a state—in Napoleon's empire or, in his later view, in the Prussian state, both of which represent only the precursors of the universal state of the future that will embrace the whole of humanity. For Marx, on the contrary, the development leads by way of social revolution and a transitional dictatorship of the proletariat to a radical withering away of the state— that is, to a radical elimination of the division of labor and its accompanying political superstructure of classes, states, and wars —and thus to the uniting of the earth in a "society of free men."

This contrast is more than just a difference of terminology. It is true that both Hegel and Marx refer to the final situation as one in which the general and the particular, the public and the private, the citizen and the private individual will be reconciled and balanced. But this final reconciliation is seen from opposite angles. Hegel sees it as a commitment of mankind to those "great objects, great aims, great contents" of a public nature on which, in his view, all private fortune and all private choice depend. Marx, on the contrary, sees it as a completely unlimited unfolding and development of just this private fortune and private choice. In the passage of *The German Ideology* (1846) in which he depicts the coming Communistic society in greatest detail, Marx refers to it as one in which each individual, "instead of having an exclusive field of activity . . . can develop himself in whatever branches he likes, with society regulating general production and by this very means enabling me to do this today and that tomorrow, to hunt in the morning, fish in the afternoon, carry on animal husbandry in the evening, and even criticize the food without ever actually becoming a hunter, a fisherman, a herdsman, or a critic."

These similarities and differences are particularly relevant to Hegel's and Marx's encounters with the problem of power, a central element in both of their systems. Both perceive that mankind's development to freedom inevitably involves the development of power. Hegel, indeed, went beyond this point and became the first to recognize the accompanying problem that we discussed in our opening chapter—namely, the tendency of man's creations to harden into a "stiff and hostile objectivity" which, in the form of "external rules" and "mechanical customs," is prone to turn against man and imprison him anew in its bonds.

This tendency of man's creations to make themselves independent and subject him to a bondage from which he must then break free anew was seen by Hegel as the basic dynamic law of human development. Progress, in Hegel's mind, necessarily took the form of a laborious struggle against obstacles. Only through blood and tears, sweat and toil could something be truly brought into being by man. Progress was achieved only when the negative fetters set up by man's previous efforts were torn down again and something more appropriate achieved. Progress, in other words, could not occur in a straight line but only through a process of twice-repeated negation. This zigzag movement—the original setting up of something positive which in turn became a fetter, the negation and the breaking of that fetter (or the negation of negation), and its replacement by a new and more advanced positive thing—was the original concrete experience that gave Hegel the inspiration for his whole theory of dialectics.

The dialectical pattern that Hegel thus derived from the conditions of his own age was extended by him to the whole course of world history and, beyond that, to the evolution of the entire universe. The strangeness of Hegel's view of world history, its curious mixture of abstract speculation with penetrating interpretation of quite concrete historical processes, and its patent arbitrariness should not obscure the greatness of his aspirations or the real value of his insights. At a time when Western civilization was increasingly being split apart by a wide variety of subjective drives—religious, political, economic, philosophic, scientific—and when the results of these drives were already beginning to consolidate themselves into a "counterpower" that men no longer understood or controlled, Hegel singlehandedly attempted to restore the situation. By coordinating all these different subjective drives in his new dialectical method, he sought to re-establish men's understanding and control over the objective world that was in process of creation. Having grasped the essentially two-sided character of power, he strove, through the responsible understanding and control of power, to safeguard human freedom.

A generation later, Marx took up where Hegel had left off. He, too, was to place the process of "alienation" (the term he took over from Hegel to describe the inherent antagonism between man and his works) at the center of his interpretation. But Marx's generation in the 1840's faced a quite different situation from that of Hegel. The industrial revolution, of which Hegel had observed only the beginnings, had by then completed its first great spurt. For Marx, the problem was no longer merely the general tendency of man's works to become solidified into "external rules" and "mechanical customs." The problem was now posed in much more specific terms as the industrial revolution increasingly crystallized into an alien industrial civilization in which man's natural development seemed threatened at every turn. The increasing momentum and complexity of this new society, its tendency to consolidate itself into counterpower, and its consequent threat to the further development of human freedom formed the starting point of Marx's analysis, the main stages of which are found in his "Paris manuscripts" of 1844 and *The German Ideology* a couple of years later.

Marx's approach to the industrial society of his time differed quite radically from the views of other critics like Owen, Saint-Simon, Proudhon, and Bakunin. Like Hegel, he was inclined to see in this society not so much a problem of socio-economic relations or exploitation as a problem of power, and of the inevitable two-sidedness of all power processes. To him the new industrial order was the supreme manifestation of the objective counterpower that men brought into being through their own efforts to advance themselves. Industrial society appeared to Marx as an all-comprehensive system of constraint affecting not only men's bodies but, equally and even more profoundly, their souls. He saw its powerful forces pressing down on all members of society, capitalists and proletarians alike. But it was his thesis that the capitalists, being favored by the system, did not realize this fatal distortion, whereas the proletarians, on whom its full force was centered, could be made to realize and ultimately to correct it.

In thus interpreting the new world of industrialized society in terms of the power that represented its central characteristic, Marx achieved an insight whose importance can hardly be over-estimated. Yet because he failed to realize the full scope and complexity of the phenomena he was dealing with, he achieved this insight in so incomplete and distorted a manner that the whole of his subsequent analysis was to be correspondingly distorted. Marx's fundamental error lay in confusing certain incidental aspects of the industrial society of his time—primarily its capitalist form of organization—with the essential problems that are present in all industrial societies and arise directly from the tremendous growth of power that takes place in them.

In reality, the industrial revolution had raised two distinct types of problems as it hurried mankind forward from the agricultural phase of his development into a stage that is characterized by this incomparably higher level of power. On the one hand, it raised basic and hitherto unknown problems with respect to the recognition and control of this power—problems that were to be the same for all industrial societies, whatever their economic organization happened to be. At the same time, it also raised limited, more or less accidental and transient problems associated with its particular capitalist form of organization. Marx, instead of focusing his attention on the former type of issues and the problems of safeguarding human freedom under the general conditions of industrialism, chose to attribute all the evils of industrial society to the capitalist organization that prevailed in the industrial society of his own day. He thus arrived at the fatal error of viewing the fundamental problems of the industrial era as something whose resolution did not require any transformation of the structure of industry itself but simply the replacement of its capitalistic economic form with a Communistic one.

As a result of this one-sided definition of the problem, Marx was led to two further inferences whose groundlessness is by now only too apparent. The first was his belief that the course of development could not be effectively transformed by gradualist and democratic means but only by a world revolution which would break up and sweep away the basic power structure of existing societies. The second was his assumption that such a world revolution, by superseding the existing class relationships, would bring the existing phase of world history (or "pre-history," as he called it) to a close and usher in a new, essentially posthistorical order in which dialectical processes would no longer operate and there would be neither power nor counterpower.

Such a state of affairs, Marx conceded, would not come about all at once. The dictatorship of the proletariat to be set up by the world revolution would still be an organization based on power, a state. Only after a transitional period of short but not clearly defined duration would mankind be ready for the truly radical step. This would be nothing less than a changeover from the dictatorship of the proletariat to the "society of free men," from a community based upon power, held together and controlled by power, to a stateless society in which all elements of force and constraint would wither away and "crude Communism" would be transformed into "true Communism."

Thus Marx, having started out like Hegel from the recognition of power and the more and more complex problems it raised, did not end up as Hegel had done with the demand that this power be submitted to responsible control. On the contrary, he seems to have envisaged the radical elimination of all control whatsoever. True, he says at one point in *The German Ideology* that the Communist revolution will bring about "the control and conscious regulation of these powers, born of the reciprocal interactions of men, which have hitherto imposed upon and ruled them as completely alien powers." Yet as a practical matter, the society of free men that he postulated as the ultimate stage of man's quest for freedom was to be so completely stripped of all controls that one cannot see how it was supposed even to hold together, far less to function.

This inconceivable picture of an uncontrolled industrial society could have been arrived at only by way of a set of assumptions about power that ran directly counter to all previous experience, as well as to all development since Marx's time. In the first place, Marx conceived his new society as based on a fundamental separation between civilian-industrial power on the one hand and political-military power on the other. He warmly endorsed the former type of power. The industrial revolution with its benefits was to be consummated by the society of free men. But political-military power, the state, in which he saw only the instrument of class warfare and oppression, was to be entirely eliminated. Thus

Marx arrived at a society that was self-contradictory in its very essence—a society that would be continually building up civilian-industrial power while lacking the political power to coordinate and control it.

In the second place, Marx assumed that the power inherent in the emerging industrial civilization would continue to be as easy to administer as it seemed to be in its beginnings. At a time when neither their dynamism nor their complexity had really developed, Marx could take a most naïve view of the amount of co-ordination and control that would be needed to run the new industrial societies. He could still believe that with the elimination of the outward forms of power—private property, class structures, the state, the bureaucracy—there could come into being an idyllic society in which everybody would freely indulge in different activities and in which "rule over people" would reduce itself to a mere "administration of things."

However deep the contrasts between their conceptions of man and his development, both Hegel and Marx are characteristically agreed in representing this development as one that is destined to come to rest in a final conclusion. In this way they both reveal that, while aware of the decisive change that occurred with the breakthrough into the modern era, they have only half grasped its real significance. With one foot they have stepped across the chasm between the static conceptions of the agricultural period and the dynamic ones of the industrial period; with the other they still remain rooted in the earlier era. They have understood that man is not a static being but one whose essence lies in the ability to surpass himself, to develop, and that his natural capabilities can only gradually realize themselves in the course of this development. At the same time, their belief that this development will stop with themselves stamps both Hegel and Marx as characteristic representatives of the transitional period between the agricultural and the industrial stage, between an essentially static and an essentially dynamic existence.

Hegel and Marx are both convinced that while the development of mankind is a process directed to a goal, it is still a limited process whose goal they have identified and brought to consciousness through their own analysis. Both of them are convinced that with the attainment of this goal, whether it be the universal state or the universal society, the contradictions between man and nature, between the public and private spheres, between the individual as citizen and the individual as private person, will be overcome and the development of mankind will arrive at a permanent conclusion. Both are convinced that with the attainment of this goal mankind will have solved its fundamental problems and arrived at a level of existence on which it will thereafter continue to exist undisturbed for all eternity. Thus for both of them the development of man is simply an episode filled with movement, beyond which mankind will enter into a permanent condition devoid of further movement.

In other words, both Hegel and Marx begin by bringing out the basically historical character of man's existence, only to yield to the overpowering influence of the intellectual tradition of the agricultural era and reincorporate it into an unhistorical, static conception. The historical development of mankind is confined by them to a limited phase; at its close the contradictions that have developed in its course will be resolved permanently in a basic reconciliation of a sort that is entirely consistent with the traditional conceptions of harmony of the agricultural period.

With this half insight, they obscure the fact that the development of mankind is actually not a limited but an unending process, one that has no more come to a halt with their systems than it did with any of the earlier ones. Above all, they obscure the most fundamental problem involved in this continuing, endless development of mankind; the fact, namely, that this development, which begins with a radical separation of man from his animal origins, in his "pushing off" from nature, must necessarily lead to an ever-increasing extension of this separation between man and nature as the development continues. In other words, they obscure the fact that the problems raised by this constantly increasing separation of man from nature cannot be solved once for all but can only be clarified from case to case and provisionally overcome in an endless succession of partial solutions.

4

Power in Industrial
Civilizations

SINCE THE OUTBREAK of the First World War in 1914,
the whole of human existence has been more profoundly transformed than Hegel or Marx could
possibly have foreseen—more profoundly, in fact, than at any time
in the preceding half-million years. Our passage from the agricultural into the industrial stage of man's development involves
a far more fundamental upheaval than our forebears' advance
from hunting to agriculture some ten thousand years ago. Con-
sidering the radical nature of the changes in which we are now
caught up, the whole of the so-called modern era that began with
the Renaissance may be justifiably regarded as no more than a transitional period in which the familiar patterns of the agricultural
stage were gradually being undermined and disrupted by the new
forces described in the preceding chapter. The centuries to which
we conventionally accord the name of "modern" actually represent the closing phase of the agricultural epoch that had begun
around 8000 B.C. with man's original adoption of a settled existence based on cultivation of the soil. What is really, fundamen-

tally new in man's experience is not the modern era but rather the industrial stage for which it prepared the way and on which we are now embarked.

The End of Modern Times

Throughout the whole extent of this modern era, Western civilization had found itself increasingly involved in a far-reaching process of transformation in virtually every field—religion and philosophy, state and society, ways of life and attitudes toward life. And yet this transformation remained to the very end within the traditional cultural setting of the agricultural period. As the state consolidated itself, its form at first remained overwhelmingly monarchical. Modern society developed within the mold of the established feudal-hierarchical order. The economy grew by leaps and bounds, yet both the productive relationships and the general way of life remained within the familiar framework that had existed for thousands of years. Although the static attitude of society as a whole was increasingly being transformed into a dynamic one, the weight of inherited habits of thought continued to impede the full unfolding of this new dynamism. While the intellectual, political, and social structure of Western civilization was being more and more shaken and undermined, its main characteristics appeared to remain intact. Up to the early years of our own century, Western civilization everywhere continued to exhibit the traditional physiognomy of the agricultural stage.

In view of the excessive duration of this transitional period and the depth of the changes that were in the making, the breakthrough, when it came, was bound to assume dramatic forms. The four brief years of the First World War sufficed to sweep the long enfeebled cultural system of the agricultural period into the discard. Its main pillar, the institution of personal monarchy, was decisively shaken. No fewer than five of the most ancient and powerful ruling houses—the Hapsburgs, the Hohenzollerns, the Romanovs, the Ottoman Sultans, and the Manchu dynasty in

China—fell one after the other. With the ruling houses fell also the feudal-hierarchical order of society that had been so intimately bound up with them. Democracy, undergirded by industrial mass production, became the generally accepted form both politically and socially. With it went a far-reaching equalization in the position of the sexes. The political, economic, and social upheavals through which these changes were accomplished knocked irreparable breaches in the traditional attitudes and ways of thought. With the establishment of the League of Nations and, after 1945, of the much more comprehensive United Nations organization, the world for the first time began to assume the character of a single political order.

While these changes elude any simple explanation, it is obvious that the principal force behind them was the progress of the industrial revolution as it spread outward from its original centers in the West and, at the same time, assumed an increasingly intensified form in the countries where it had developed originally. These trends, in turn, would have been inconceivable without the world-wide increase in population which first became apparent in the late eighteenth century and which still continues virtually unchecked nearly two hundred years later. From around the middle of the nineteenth century, progressive improvements in medicine and sanitation began to show their effects on a considerable scale, first in the industrialized countries of the West but to an increasing extent in the non-Western areas as well. Between 1850 and 1900, world population rose by almost 50 per cent, to some 1.6 billion. The population of Europe alone, which had stood at some 187 million in 1800, had increased to 266 million in 1850, 401 million in 1900, 460 million on the eve of the First World War, and 560 million in 1950.

Slower to experience this demographic trend were the great Asian agricultural areas that had been the centers of world population since the time of the earliest High Civilizations. Throughout the nineteenth and into the twentieth century, population growth in India, China, and elsewhere was held back by recurrent famines, epidemics, and civil strife. By the mid-twentieth century, however, these areas were strongly reasserting their demographic lead. In India, where up to 1921 the population had advanced slowly or even declined, it now tended to leap ahead each decade. Even more formidable, both absolutely and relatively, was the increase in the population of mainland China, whose own phenomenal rate of increase was considerably surpassed by Ceylon, Thailand, and Malaya as well as many of the Latin American countries. Thus the East, which for as far as we can look back has always been more densely populated than the West, has tended to become ever more populous and congested. Opportunities for the relief of overpopulation, whether by migration overseas or by internal migration to the new industrial centers, remained severely limited. Where such migration did occur, it took place under conditions of extreme privation far surpassing those experienced in the initial period of industrialization in Western countries.

Meanwhile the industrial revolution has conquered the world. From a movement originally nurtured by and confined to Western civilization, it has become the chief transforming agent of all the other contemporary world civilizations. Though everywhere similar in its purely technical aspects, industrialization reflected an astonishing multiplicity of impulses and motives as it extended its conquests to one after another of the world's traditional societies. In Western Europe and North America it was, as we have already indicated, essentially a private affair. Countless individuals, seeking only their private advantage, seized upon the opportunities that were opening up and, by the cumulative effect of their individual, self-serving activities, gave the process the drive and the dynamism that were to transform first the economic life of their countries and eventually the whole pattern of existence.

Once the change to an industrial civilization had been successfully initiated in the West, a similar process was undertaken in other parts of the world—but often for quite different reasons and with widely differing methods. In Japan, a handful of far-seeing nineteenth-century statesmen, determined to equip their country to hold its own against the might of the Western powers, imposed upon their native civilization a Western industrial superstructure that at first was almost wholly state-inspired. Private civilian interests emerged only gradually to a position of independent leadership. Handicraft industries continued to flourish and expand side by side with the development of modern heavy industries.

In Russia, the break with the essentially private pattern of Western industrial civilization after the Bolshevik Revolution of 1917 was incomparably more radical. Here a revolutionary dictatorship deliberately imposed industrialization upon the entire society in a conscious effort to meet and eventually overcome the Western, capitalist form of industrial organization. The transformation of Soviet society, within little more than a generation, from its traditional and still predominantly rural structure into a modern, industrialized and increasingly urban society, was entirely state-planned, state-directed, and imposed upon the Soviet peoples by an unprecedented system of coercion that bore scant resemblance to Marx's vision of a society freed from exploitation and constraint. Communist China in the years since 1949 has embarked upon a similar process from an even more primitive base and by still more ruthless methods.

In India and the other countries that have achieved independence from Western rule in the years since 1945, industrialization has been inspired by still other motives. Here it represents in part a simple endeavor to relieve an extremity of material need and to begin, by the quickest methods available, to make some provision for coming generations. In addition, powerful emotional considerations have here come into play. The success of the Western powers in establishing their domination over Oriental peoples in the course of the modern era was largely due to the fact that they had so far outstripped the latter in industrial development. Western colonialism had affected the peoples of the great Oriental civilizations in their most vital spot, their pride in their own cultural superiority. In order to vindicate their personal and racial dignity, the peoples of Asia and Africa were bound to press for a full assertion of racial and cultural equality as soon as the opportunity arose.

Industrialization thus acquired for these peoples a symbolic value that frequently overshadowed its material significance. Political independence alone, they came to feel, was insufficient and precarious. Only when it was supplemented and fortified by industrialization—especially the establishment of heavy industry—would the balance be truly restored.

Understandable as this attitude undoubtedly is, it reflects a notion of industrial processes that was already tending to become obsolete at the very time it was formulated. Instead of the finite process that Hegel and Marx had imagined, the industrial revolution has revealed itself to the eyes of the twentieth century as a movement that actually knows no limits but seems destined to develop in greater and greater complexity and at ever-increasing speeds as far ahead as we can see. The task that the Asian and African countries have actually set themselves, therefore, is not merely to catch up with one economic revolution which has passed them by, but to catch up with a second and far more complex phase of industrial development as well. Apart from Japan, India, and China, it may be questioned whether any of these countries possesses the material basis or the scientific and technological requisites that would enable it to embark successfully upon this new and higher phase of industrialization.

The Structure of Industrial Society

Thus it is the West that has pioneered the breakthrough into the fully industrialized stage of human development, just as it earlier led the breakthrough from the static conditions of traditional agricultural society into the increasing turmoil of the modern era. The beginnings of this new stage go back to a far-reaching change in the character and direction of the industrial revolution that first became fully apparent at about the time of the First

World War, although its origins reach back several decades earlier.

Since the late nineteenth century, the dynamic trends inherent in the process of industrialization in the original industrialized countries had been further intensified by a new and conscious systematization of efforts in many fields. Improved methods and processes were introduced in established industries, and similar methods were extended into new fields, such as the electrical and chemical industries, which required a far more solid and comprehensive theoretical basis. The self-taught pioneers who had directed the original industrial revolution began to be replaced by academically trained engineers and chemists and, at the top, by far-seeing financiers and industrial organizers. Thus the way was paved for a general change-over from the technological to the scientific approach in industrial development, from accidental discoveries to systematic innovation through organized research efforts.

A related and equally radical change was the expansion in the size of industrial establishments and the corresponding transformation in methods of production. In general, the decisive shift to mass-production methods began to be apparent only around the beginning of the twentieth century, and was greatly intensified from 1914 onward in response to wartime demands. It was not until the First World War that the iron and steel industry began making extensive use of mass-production methods, which thereafter were rapidly adopted by industry generally.

In the meantime the leisurely pace and limited scope that had characterized the industrial revolution in its earlier stages was beginning to give way to the rapidly changing and massive character that has made its continued expansion the dominant force of our age. Within our own lifetime, industrial production has expanded from a limited number of fields to virtually all fields, at the same time achieving an almost unbelievable growth in the sheer volume of output. The details of this process are widely familiar: the vast increase in the use of energy, much of it from new sources such as oil and water power; the staggering growth in steel production, in Europe and North America and to an increasing extent in other parts of the world; the even more revolutionary development of the chemical industry and, more recently, the appearance of wholly new synthetic products, the result of research carried on mainly in the years since the Second World War; the more and more prevalent use of assembly-line techniques and, again in recent years, of automated processes.

The key to this whole development has been the systematic application of the scientific approach and of scientific methods, not only in industry *per se* but universally, in matters of social organization and distribution, in agriculture as well as in industry. In all of these fields, moreover, science has gradually tended to change its function. From a mere tool for use in established processes, it has become the inspiration for new discoveries and processes. Electronics and nuclear physics present the most familiar instances in which science has become not just the handmaiden of progress but its actual promoter, opening up by its discoveries new perspectives and wholly different fields of practical application.

This profound alteration in the character and scope of industrial processes has been accompanied by an equally far-reaching change in the forms of economic ownership and administration. Here again, the situation that confronts us today has altered almost beyond recognition from that of only a few decades ago. In the course of our own lifetimes the classical type of capitalist entrepreneur has been replaced by a corporation, a professional business hierarchy. These modern corporations are striking illustrations of what we may call objective economic power—vast entities that have become increasingly divorced from, and independent of, the stockholders who represented their original economic base. Continuity of direction in these huge organizations is maintained by internal selection, by succession within the group, rather than through election by the nominal proprietors, the stockholders.

The growth of these giant corporations has increasingly blurred the historical distinction between the public and private spheres. Their influence permeates the whole of society in a manner previously possible only to governments. At the same time, considerations of public interest and policy have come to play a significant role even within these citadels of the "private" sphere. Like the classic owner-entrepreneur, the modern corporation is still concerned with profits, but no longer to the exclusion of other considerations. The self-interest that animates it is no longer the simple, individual self-interest of the classical "economic man," but that of a vast collective entity which reaches into every stratum of society and exerts an influence comparable to that of the state itself. Much the same is true of their counterparts, the great labor organizations that have increasingly institutionalized the aspirations of the individual worker whose interests they purport to represent. Meanwhile the state itself has enormously expanded the scope of its activity in response to the growing magnitude, complexity, and competing interests of industrial society.

A further characteristic of the advanced industrial society as we know it today is the development of mass consumption as a central feature of economic life. Professor W. W. Rostow, in his celebrated treatise *The Stages of Economic Growth,* has vividly reminded us how the conditions of life have been transformed over the past half-century or so, first in North America and more recently in Western Europe and Japan, by the development of the consumer industries and the resultant improvement in the material conditions of existence if not in its quality and tone. Equally characteristic of the advance to a mass-consumption society has been the unrestrained development of new advertising and selling techniques. The supermarket, the mail-order house, the radio and later the television commercial, the mass and sophistication of promotion and advertisement in newspapers and magazines, are concomitants of the mass society as it has evolved in the United States and, with some variations, is now tending to evolve elsewhere.

But the most profoundly characteristic feature of our industrial mass societies has been the steady influx of population into the great industrial areas and the resultant growth of those large-scale industrial concentrations that give our contemporary civilization its typical structure and form. In contrast to the 70 to 80 per cent of the population tied down to food production in the traditional agricultural societies, by the mid-twentieth century the proportion engaged in agricultural pursuits had been reduced to around 50 per cent in the Soviet Union and Japan, and to 12 per cent or less in Europe and North America. In the latter area, the growing application of industrial methods to agriculture not only sufficed to satisfy the alimentary needs of the entire population but resulted in a piling up of surpluses far in excess of national requirements.

With their huge manufacturing plants and their accompanying nexus of rail and road networks, power grids, ports, banking systems, and the like, the full-fledged urban concentrations that form the backbone of the new industrial society are quite unlike the localized, largely self-sufficient urban units of the pre-industrial era. Like luxuriant tropical vegetation, they have developed into immensely complex systems of production and distribution that integrate whole regions, countries, and even continents into almost inextricable networks of productive relationships.

These intricately intermeshed, mass concentrations of people and facilities have shaped our economic and social life into something radically different from the diffuse civilizations of earlier times. The lodging, feeding, and transporting of these concentrations of people, their amusement and recreation have been made possible only through the development of a new kind of mass-organized coexistence, a new way of life that breeds its own mental outlook—impersonal, alert, intense. From the urban centers this characteristic atmosphere has spread outward to permeate our whole society. Even the modern farmer has tended to become an agricultural businessman, far more attuned to the outlook of his urban contemporaries than to that of his rural forefathers with their intimate identification with the cycle of natural processes.

Modern industrial societies are nothing like the "accidental masses" studied by Gustave Le Bon in his classic nineteenth-century analysis of *The Crowd*. On the contrary, they are highly organized institutional complexes that somehow manage to integrate vast numbers of people with widely differing personalities, activities, and objectives into viable and effective combinations. These interweaving patterns of social and economic relationships have become so extensive and so complicated that they can be kept going only by mass-organization procedures. They have developed into veritable rabbit warrens of interrelations of every conceivable kind. Superimposed on the basic occupational relationships are an unprecedented array of highly articulated social, administrative, and political institutions.

In this process, the human masses that represent the raw material of our urban societies have also been organized and disciplined into closely institutionalized hierarchies. The individual, as such writers as William H. Whyte and C. Wright Mills have pointed out, is integrated with an inexorable pressure into these vast social machineries. Whatever the differences in ideology, spirit, and methods from one industrialized country to another, the power of the social structure itself has become so overwhelming that it closely governs the individual's personal fate as well as his relations with his fellows. Procedures tend to become more and more formalized and stereotyped. The "other-directed" person, in David Riesman's phrase, is becoming more and more prevalent; the "inner-directed" man is in constant danger of being squeezed out.

From this point of view, there is comparatively little difference between the mass societies of the democratic world and those that have developed in the Soviet Union and other Communist states. However different in inspiration and guiding spirit, both types of society have tended to take on similar characteristics in response to similar exigencies. The industrialization of the Soviet Union in the 1920's and 1930's required a radical departure from the traditional easygoing ways of the old Russia and the introduction of the quite novel habits of labor discipline, punctuality, and neatness, care of public property, and "bourgeois" family ethics required by modern industrial societies. Indeed, the bureaucratic apparatus of Communism is even more highly elaborated and all-pervasive than that of capitalist societies, since it includes not only the state or managerial hierarchies dealing with administration and production but also the parallel organizations designed to assure the control of the ruling party over virtually all sectors of the people's lives and activities.

In summary, our contemporary industrial civilization, whether "capitalist" or "socialist" in its ideological inspiration, is everywhere characterized by an unprecedented degree of organization that extends itself throughout the vast and intricate network of human activities. In the mass societies of today this had to be so. The old, simple structures, the free choices of earlier ages, have become completely unworkable. Our industrial mass societies can function only by processes of mass organization. We live in a world in which every form of political and economic activity, every aspect of our social lives, all types of study and education, and almost every form of leisure have tended to become mass organized. The institutionalization of modern society has become well-nigh total.

THE NEMESIS OF RATIONALITY

There is no need to be entirely negative in judging the fruits of industrialization as manifested in the contemporary mass society. Though it inevitably tends toward an excessive degree of "institutionalization" and "massification," industrialization has also proved itself a liberating and stimulating force of a character quite new to man's experience. In our nostalgia for the depth and organic unity of the older civilizations, we are apt to forget that these qualities were achieved only at the cost of narrow and harsh restrictions, within a strait jacket of traditional patterns which ran counter to every requirement of human justice and, once established, were exceedingly difficult to change. Great as they undoubtedly were, these earlier cultural achievements were almost invariably the jealously guarded preserve of a ruling minority that alone fully shared in and enjoyed them. The vast majority of the people were suppressed or excluded on varying grounds of sex, class, caste, or race.

This is not nearly so true of the mass civilizations of today. Industrialization has not only showered us with a rain of material benefits and resources beyond our wildest dreams; it has also torn down or is in the process of tearing down traditional restrictions of class and sex and thereby making its benefits available to all the people rather than just a few. If it tends to "overorganize" the individual, it has also given him much more freedom to develop his mind and abilities and to better himself both economically and socially.

Characteristic of this changed climate are the rapid and sweeping political changes that have accompanied the triumph of the new industrial civilizations and supplanted the hierarchic political and social systems that in many countries had persisted throughout the eighteenth and nineteenth centuries. Universal suffrage, a rare exception before 1918, has become so much the accepted form that even reactionary and totalitarian governments have had to pay at least lip service to it. Parallel with this political emancipation of the masses, women have secured equality with men at least in principle, although much more slowly in practice.

The achievement of independence by the majority of the peoples of Asia and Africa in the years since 1945 not only has restored the political dignity of many millions of formerly subject peoples but has gone a long way toward removing the "color bar" that around 1900 was perhaps more widespread and accentuated than at any earlier time. The action of the government of India in banning the caste system, with its age-old discriminations and restrictions, is another major step in this liberating process. In the United States, the processes set in motion by the 1954 Supreme Court decision outlawing racial discrimination in education re-

flect a similar tendency to eliminate disabilities that can no longer
be squared with prevailing political and social demands.

Furthermore, the combination of great concentrations of people
and industrial power with an ever-growing diversity and specialization of function has given the mass societies of our contemporary industrial civilization an almost irresistible impact. The
tremendous capacity for "getting things done," inherent in this
type of social organization, was first disclosed by the industrial
mobilizations of the two World Wars, when the energies of the
belligerent countries, normally diffused in a variety of civilian
endeavors, were for the first time brought into line and sharply
focused upon common tasks and targets. This mobilization of
energy was particularly conspicuous in the American war effort of
1941–45, in which standards of home consumption were maintained and even increased at the very time when war production
was being built up to a level surpassing that of friend and foe
combined—and without stretching manpower or productive capacity to anything like its full potential.

Deeply impressive as is this capacity for mass effort, however, it
is subject to very important and potentially critical weaknesses,
some of which are obvious while others have remained virtually
unnoticed. Their roots lie far back in the process of man's development; some of them, indeed, go all the way back to that
initial break with nature that we have identified as the starting
point of his specifically human career.

We have already seen that in establishing his independence of
nature and setting out to transform the world by the exercise of
his own subjective power, man has tended to involve himself in
new forms of "cultural" bondage which are imposed upon him
by the objective power of his own works. This process has reached
a culminating point in the industrial societies of our time. The
uninhibited exercise of man's rational faculties, as he has applied
them to the building up of industrial civilization, has brought
about a situation that is in essential respects the reverse of rational. Just as power tends to turn into counterpower, rationality

has tended to turn into irrationality. In pursuing his independence of nature, man has produced a state of affairs that is in the most fundamental sense contrary to nature itself.

Let us recall for a moment that man, in creating the works by which he seeks to free himself from the bondage of nature, creates two types of power. He creates a power of which he is conscious, and for which he is bound to feel responsibility. And, at the same time, he creates a hidden power of which he is normally not aware at all, a power that completely ties him with its bonds, guides him in its paths, reshapes his feeling and thinking, and determines his perspectives and horizons without his having the remotest suspicion of what is happening to him.

This hidden side of the problem of power could be largely ignored so long as man's activities remained essentially within a "natural" framework. The rationality of man developed only very slowly and partially, and for a long time displayed no real durability. Man on the whole was able to exercise an adequate measure of control over the works he created. These works, the refashioning of the landscape, its settlements, its institutions and spiritual achievements, were the product of his natural forces and were adapted to his normal capacities. He could keep an over-all view of them, could find his bearings among them, could even remodel them without undue difficulty when their objective power resisted him. Even their rationality was limited. They were incorporated into nature, not set against nature.

Even when man increasingly intervened in and reconstituted it, nature still remained his environment, to whose requirements and rhythms his own nature was adapted. Amid all its transformations, his world remained a "natural" world. His attempts to reform it remained partial in character, mere man-made enclaves in the natural environment, and always in danger of breaking down and reverting to nature. Their maintenance required a continuing effort; and, even so, all of the different civilizations experienced periods of breakdown in which a part of the cultural inheritance was lost.

With the transition to the industrial stage, however, the relationship of man to his works was altered from the ground up. Thanks to the immensely increased productivity of the industrial civilization, man's cultural achievements were not only assured and preserved but multiplied themselves in steadily increasing measure. Accumulating at the centers of the new civilization, the great interchange points and administrative centers, they spread out and solidified more and more into a closed and consistent world of their own. With this consolidation, the relationship of man to his works was reversed. It was no longer man who imposed his partial and limited rationality on his works, but the industrial world with its consolidated works that imposed *its* rationality, *its* logic, on him. Man, who had thus far been largely his own master, was compelled to adapt himself to the way of life that his own works required.

In this way the industrial world increasingly began to interpose itself between nature on one side and man on the other. This man-made industrial world, however, is a completely artificial world whose inner structure makes it something entirely new. As a product of human reason, it is rational through and through. Built up exclusively on rational principles, it seeks throughout its structure to realize its aims in entirely rational—that is, in the shortest and most economical—ways. In all its parts it represents a "frozen rationality." As an artificial construction, it has neither a natural adaptability to circumstances nor a natural capacity for regeneration, for the spontaneous healing of damages. In other words, it is simply the objectification of the completely rational capacity of man—as distinguished from the interweaving of irrational and rational elements that constitutes man's natural inheritance.

With their highly complex, interrelated structures, these industrial mass societies are incomparably more vulnerable to disturbance of any kind than were their less complex and coordinated predecessors. The same specialization and integration that so vastly increase their power when everything is working properly have made them correspondingly susceptible to the effects of any mishap. The greater the degree of integration of the system, of its dependence on such key units as power dams, specialized plants, railroad centers, and ports, the greater the danger that the crippling of one or more of its elements may lead eventually to a breakdown of the entire network.

It is true that the enormous resources developed in industrial society provide reserves which normally make it possible to surmount even very widespread and severe disruptions. The two World Wars revealed unsuspected powers of improvisation that repeatedly confounded the prophets of breakdown. Yet the same experience also showed that this resiliency and ability to improvise have definite limits. Even the victorious powers in the Second World War repeatedly approached the verge of collapse as the result of submarine warfare or, in the case of Britain, air bombardment. The experience of Germany and Japan under concentrated air attack shows what can happen to an industrialized society if its powers of control and recuperation are worn down beyond a certain critical point. Physical damage on the spot is then compounded by functional disruption throughout the system, until the result is either a dangerous weakening or, in the extreme case, total collapse.

But the possibility of breakdown in contemporary industrial society is not limited to the extreme contingency of attack from without. It is inherent in the structure of the society itself. In its stiff and inflexible rationality, the industrial world opposes itself to nature in precisely those aspects in which nature itself is most irrational—for example, the weather. The life process of a great modern city or industrial area consists of a thoroughly rationalized network of subordinate processes of all kinds. The rationality of this life process can be gravely disturbed by large-scale meteorological changes. A heavy snowfall, for example, can paralyze a great city. Especially dependent on the moods of nature are transport and communications, above all air transport, the very branch in which man has raised himself farthest above the limitations imposed by nature.

The uncompromising rationality of industrial processes collides with the irrationality of nature in many other points as well. Nature, as we see more and more, is based not on simple, static foundations but on internally equilibrated processes such as we see in ecology. Wherever man, with his sense of direct action, interferes in such balanced processes, he not only disturbs them but makes their equilibrium difficult if not impossible to restore.

Another such tension between nature and the industrial world is found in the problem of natural resources. The functioning of the industrial world imperatively requires raw materials, in a tremendously increased measure compared with all former epochs, and, moreover, in a constantly increasing measure. Thus far the problem has not become really acute, partly because better production or research processes have repeatedly modified current requirements, partly because of the possibilities of transformation opened up by nuclear chemistry. But this is true only for the world as a whole. In particular areas serious problems have already arisen. In terms of centuries one cannot overlook the possibilities of serious conflict arising from the depletion of raw material sources.

But it is not only in its contacts with nature that the world of industrial civilization encounters problems of this order. Similar problems are encountered in its own way of functioning. These difficulties can best be observed where the industrial civilization has attained its highest degree of organization, in the great industrial concerns. Standing at a pinnacle of the highest rationality, it is precisely these great organizations that demonstrate most clearly the limitations of a purely rationalistic approach. The rationality of organization and methods does not guarantee the rationality of the actual processes. For these latter do not accomplish themselves mechanically. At the decisive points of concentration they demand comprehensive oversights and decisions that must be taken on the basis not of rational but of irrational faculties. At their decisive stages, in other words, these processes require hierarchies of people capable of making decisions.

The capacities of men for achieving such oversights and making such decisions are, however, decidedly limited. Where this measure is exceeded, man's natural decision-making capabilities are overstrained and, in place of a clearly overseen situation and a resultant clear decision, we get a purely mechanical decision. It is true that this process can be eased by replacing individual with collective decisions (which, however, invariably have their own drawbacks), and also by the development of whole batteries of computers, mechanical tabulations and indices. But these still remain mechanical aids. They can support the actual decision; they cannot replace it. The fact is that in these great industrial organizations the rationality of man has precipitated and objectively solidified itself on a scale which surpasses man's natural capacities many times over.

The result of all this is not that the machinery actually breaks down. That happens only in quite extreme cases, if at all. What does happen is that the organization increasingly assimilates itself to abstract, rational models, at the same time losing concrete vitality, drive, decision, flexibility, and effectiveness. The structure remains mechanical. The different functions are mechanically joined, not organically related. The lack of clear oversight and interrelation of functions leads to overdevelopment and inflation of the apparatus, complication and delay in the conduct of business. Conversely, gaps are unperceived and important areas and points of view are disregarded.

These structural weaknesses are matched by functional ones. General oversights are difficult to achieve, especially for the longer term. Positive decisions based on inadequate general views tend to lose their lucidity, thus increasing the significance of negative decisions and omissions. A related factor arising from the complication of the modern industrial world is the long lead time and consequent delay in the testing and evaluation of a decision after it has been taken.

The artificial world of industrial civilization is as little adapted to *human* nature as it is to nature as a whole. Instead of progressively overcoming the inherent problems created by this hardening of rational structures, the conditions of industrial civilization tend to sharpen them even more. Its influence on the human beings involved tends not so much to promote the qualities required for its direction and maintenance as rather the opposite.

If the industrial world is to be maintained at a reasonable level of efficiency, it is clearly of decisive importance to develop the greatest possible number of individuals who combine great self-reliance with great scope—people who, generally speaking, have a broad horizon, can anticipate developments over the long term, and possess the ability to make critical decisions as well as the elasticity to maintain them even while promptly recognizing and effecting any necessary readjustments. In short, there is need for people with the greatest possible depth and breadth of abilities, equally endowed with highly developed irrational and rational powers, broadly cultivated and possessed of extraordinary vitality.

Yet industrial civilization tends to hamper the development of just such individuals. It does not, as in earlier, more simple and easygoing times, provide a comfortable background for the gradual unfolding of such qualities. It does not grant sufficient repose for the development of the irrational forces of the soul. Less and less does it offer the possibility of a really deep and broad cultivation.

Instead, it furthers the one-sided development of the rational faculties—and, among them, an ever sharper selection through narrow occupational specialization. It permits the individual no opportunity for rhythmical *détente* and the replenishment of his reserves of strength, but harnesses him to a work tempo of unvarying intensity. At the same time, it overwhelms him with such a mass of impressions and demands that such reserves of strength as he still has are rapidly exhausted. While it is true that advances in medicine have brought an increase in average life expectancy, we are also confronted with a vast increase in illnesses, especially heart ailments, which arise directly from this quite new psychic and physical overtension. The industrial civilization no longer affords leisure for the things that formerly served to refresh the exhausted spirit—contact with the landscape, with the general cultural inheritance, or mere sociability—or else it harnesses them into the general operation in such a way as to rob them of their former value in the relief of tension.

In this conflict between the frozen rationality of the industrial world and the spiritual forces of the human soul on which it makes such excessive demands, developments proceed in a far more unforeseen and unguided manner than is generally realized. Our world has become filled to bursting with powerful forces of every kind—people, energies, material resources, capital. This buildup of energies imparts a dynamism very like the bounce of a ball. We have been pumping our world so full of forces that it has become as difficult to handle as an inflated balloon straining at its moorings. Power is there in abundance; what is lacking is the means of controlling it at all of the various levels at which it manifests itself.

Given the superabundance of organization that characterizes our industrial society, it might seem that the problem of the co-ordination and control of power had solved itself by the development of some novel form of organization to take care of each new function as it appears. Every significant branch of activity, it seems, has been systematized and is being controlled by one means or another. Data on every conceivable subject are being amassed in enormous quantities. Governmental and private bureaucracies grow larger and more complex from year to year.

Yet the over-all impression created by this activity is highly deceptive. The mere fact that some branch of activity, or of knowledge, has been "organized" does not mean that the organization is effective, still less that it is effectively coordinated with other branches. As the power and complexity of our economic and social activities continues to grow, the danger increases that the energies involved will be not merely inadequately guided but positively misdirected. The sheer complexity and volume of the masses of people, things, facts to be dealt with almost invariably tends to result in a purely mechanical, routine form of organization that obliterates individual, qualitative distinctions and makes any real coordination extraordinarily difficult. Everywhere we find the same tendencies: wasteful duplication of efforts, overconcentration on some areas, neglect of others of equal or greater significance. In consequence, our general efficiency is reduced and any real direction is lacking.

But the real problem of the control of power in contemporary society does not lie in the organization of individual people, things, or facts, however essential. It lies in the lack of coordination at a higher level, the lack of any clear sense of over-all objectives or the means of attaining them. In building up so many different types of organizations for every conceivable purpose, we have given far too little attention to the need of coordinating and harmonizing these activities in the interests of society as a whole. Our societies are overorganized at the lower levels, undercoordinated at the higher ones. With each segment of society bent upon its own particular effort and interests, vital areas are apt to be left entirely unprovided for. Professor John Kenneth Galbraith has shown in his study of *The Affluent Society* how the American emphasis on production and still more production has tended to distort the whole structure of the economy by favoring the production of unnecessary or at best marginal goods while denying adequate resources for such vital public requirements as education, social security, housing, and national defense. The experience of the Soviet Union shows similar, if less well-publicized, departures from an optimal "social balance."

It is precisely at these higher levels, moreover, that the really great problems of industrial society present themselves: the problems of national health and education, of the balance between agriculture and industry, of urbanization and soil conservation, of national affairs and relations with other nations. And, as the Communist experience has abundantly demonstrated in recent years, mere mechanical concentration of controls is not the answer. These problems require a comprehensive perspective; yet they also require a capacity for flexible adjustment that may well involve decentralization of action.

These problems of coordination and control are all the more significant and insidious because they often fail to show up clearly. On the surface, everything is organized and "well in hand." Everything seems to be running smoothly. Slack and waste tend to go unnoticed in societies that are advancing rapidly. Yet the problems are there. Where organization remains merely external and mechanical, it cannot really control the power being generated within its area of influence with sufficient tightness or flexibility to keep it from getting out of hand.

The ways in which this can happen are widely varied. It frequently takes the form of a slow, creeping process that remains unperceived until it has reached dangerous proportions. Vast areas may become depopulated or threatened by soil erosion or undergo depreciation through lack of large-scale regional planning. It may take the form of an economic slackening off, as in France during the 1930's, of a misdirection of economic efforts or a failure to keep educational methods and facilities up to date. Again, it may take drastic forms. Normal processes may get completely out of hand and run amuck, as happened in world trade during the Great Depression or in Stalin's system of terror during his widespread purges. Or the explosive power that industrialized society builds up—politically, militarily, economically—may erupt in such indescribable international tragedy as we have twice witnessed during the past half-century.

What these catastrophes signify, however, is simply that the elements of power which are so abundantly present in contemporary industrial society have been disregarded and left uncontrolled. The rationality of the industrial world is so great that the forces it has set in motion and is constantly building up do not normally enter our consciousness at all. Mass processes of gigantic dimensions run their course as if they did not involve any power, any weight at all. The greater the power generated by the industrial civilization, the less it impresses itself on the consciousness of the people living in it.

But this objective power is nonetheless there. To a certain extent it flows along with the various processes. If, however, a chain of unfavorable circumstances one day brings about a disturbance of the normal course, the latent, invisible but gigantic power that has accumulated in our industrial civilization can suddenly become active and brush all restraints aside.

THE LOSS OF INTELLECTUAL CONTROL

We have already suggested that the remedy for this state of affairs lies not in an impossible return to the simpler conditions of the pre-industrial era, but in the growth of a spirit of awareness and responsibility which might enable us to reassert our control over the power that is constantly being generated in our industrial civilization. Unfortunately, it remains questionable whether such a spirit of awareness and responsibility has any prospect of developing within established forms of political and intellectual life.

The economic and social conditions that characterize our industrial societies have profoundly modified the form and content of political life. Modern democracy, as it developed from the seventeenth to the nineteenth centuries, had its basis in a clear-cut notion of the importance and all-round capacity of the individual citizen. This conception had reality in the much simpler conditions of the late agricultural era. The members of the body politic were supposed to be roughly equal, economically secure. They were supposed to be "self-directed," that is, to rely upon their individual consciences in making decisions and to be sufficiently well informed about the relatively simple problems confronting their communities to be able to pass fairly competent judgment upon them. Somewhat optimistically, perhaps, it was further assumed that there was a fundamental harmony between the members of a community which could be brought to light by rational discussion within small assemblies.

Today, even our democratic societies no longer exhibit these traits. Nations are now vast agglomerations of many millions of people. Even in the smallest political subdivisions, the members of the local electorate are usually far too numerous to know one another. Nor are our societies any longer composed of the upstanding, homogeneous individuals of classical democratic theory. One may or may not subscribe entirely to the prevalent view that the growth of industrial society has been accompanied by a decline in individual self-reliance and responsibility and a general deterioration of moral fiber. Political significance, in any case, has tended to shift from the individual to more or less closely organized groups—farmers, labor, white-collar workers, civil servants, etc.—into which the individual voters have been massed together.

Accompanying these changes has been an almost universal retreat from the original concept of the regulation of public affairs by the whole body of citizens. In the Communist countries and in large parts of the non-Communist world, democratic processes in the classical sense have been frankly set aside in favor of one or another form of authoritarian rule, usually sanctioned by some type of well-organized voting procedure that takes the form of an acclamation rather than a political choice. Even in those countries where democratic institutions and procedures have been most firmly established, the ordinary citizen no longer has either the ability or, in most cases, the desire to discharge the full responsibilities that democratic theory assigns to him.

For this the individual citizen is not entirely to be blamed. The great issues of our time are no longer simply matters of local knowledge, nor are they always identifiable in terms of the fundamentally "conservative" or "liberal" principles that used to serve as a rough guide to political participation. Such vital matters as the capabilities of a new weapons system, the proper balance between nuclear and conventional forces, the permissible limits of compromise in disarmament negotiations, the expediency of an increase or a reduction in taxes or tariffs, the effects of military and economic aid to the emerging nations, are extraordinarily complicated and difficult and are usually bound up with technical considerations that are quite beyond the comprehension of the ordinary layman. Even the best-informed experts seem hardly able to understand them and often take violent exception to each other's opinions in public, to the further confusion of the unenlightened citizen.

Any attempt to make such issues generally understandable is further complicated by the peculiar dangers involved in the use of mass information media, the standard means of communication and influence in mass societies. Whether publicly or privately controlled, their long-run effect is much the same. Political symbols, personalities, and issues are artificially simplified, standardized, and manipulated until they become completely banal. The whole advertising apparatus is placed at the service of the dominant clichés, repeated and repeated until they no longer carry any semblance of conviction. Not much higher in intellectual tone are the discussions of our legislative bodies, where the combination of party passion and technical ignorance or semi-ignorance too often "darkeneth counsel by words without knowledge."

Under such conditions, the average citizen has quite given up the attempt to arrive at a reasoned judgment on issues which, he instinctively feels, are beyond his comprehension as well as his ability to exert a significant influence on. He either accepts the first ready-made opinion that appeals to him or shrugs his shoulders and leaves the matter to others. This does not mean that he has given up the exercise of his political rights to any noticeable degree. On the contrary, political interest in most countries appears keener than ever. What has undergone a drastic change is the purpose and spirit of political participation. Instead of attempting to grapple responsibly with what he conceives to be the underlying issues, the average politically minded individual quite frankly tends to let himself be dominated either by his emotions, his assumed material interest, or an amalgam of the two.

This tendency serves to illustrate what is perhaps the most deeply significant and disturbing aspect of the age in which we live—the gradual loss of any adequate intellectual grasp of our over-all situation. It is true that the problems of industrial society have been engaging the attention of distinguished thinkers for the past century and a half. Yet it is highly questionable whether the full import of the changes that have been occurring has even yet been adequately comprehended, still less brought to public awareness.

The very rapidity of the transformation that has been going forward in our society raises intellectual problems that distinguish our era from any earlier period in history. The agricultural revolution, the most nearly comparable development, is generally recognized to have taken a thousand to two thousand years to run its full course. The radical transformation that began at the time of the Renaissance required roughly a hundred years for the accomplishment of its decisive initial phase. Changes in social conditions still occurred so slowly that they overlapped the life span of the individual. Each generation had time to absorb and become accustomed to the gradual modifications in its environment and manner of living. Cultural continuity was assured by the fact that the members of each new generation lived under much the same conditions as the preceding and were molded in large part by their fathers' experiences.

From the First World War onward, this kind of continuity no longer existed. That generation, swept off its feet in early youth by the repercussions of world conflict, never again found time or opportunity to take a firm footing on new ground. Since 1914, and even more noticeably since 1939, change has followed change so rapidly that we have become less and less able to keep up with these successive transformations or to understand their effects upon our lives. Successive changes have tended to blur in our consciousness, leaving us with little more than a general feeling of being caught up and rushed along by an irresistible current of new ideas and events. The effect of this transformation, unprecedented in speed, depth, comprehensiveness, and complexity, has been the abrupt snapping of the cord of continuity that ran through all man's previous intellectual experience.

A widening gap has thus been opened between our basic ideas about man and his purpose, about government and the relations between states, about social and economic relationships, and the constantly evolving conditions of our actual existence. Our religious tenets, our political and economic philosophies, our doctrines of education derive from traditions that go back for hundreds and even thousands of years. Formed under the simple and stable conditions of agricultural communities, these fundamental ideas continue to reflect the presuppositions of that type of society: the essential stability of human nature, the smallness and simplicity of the typical human group, the personal character of human relationships, the constancy of economic factors and values. They do not and cannot be expected to fit the utterly different patterns of today's mass societies.

In the absence of any systematic effort to adapt this traditional mental framework to the facts of contemporary existence, the fundamental relationship between our principles and practices has become more and more strained. The sense of continuity between past, present, and future is rapidly becoming lost. History is no longer felt as an integral and continuous process in which a living sense of the past serves as a guide to the present and a beacon for the future. Not only are we in danger of losing our sense of historical continuity; most of us are no longer even conscious of the loss.

Fewer and fewer people appear to be disturbed by the breakdown of our cultural traditions. We no longer seem to feel the need for any comprehensive understanding and control of our situation. We are in acute danger of becoming "people of the day" to whom the good and evil of each particular day is quite literally sufficient. Putting less and less effort into recovering a mastery over our fate, we have tended increasingly to surrender ourselves to the course of events in the blind hope that in some way or other it will all work out right in the end. It is certainly no accident that the favorite symbol of our age has come to be a stream, the inner stream of our thoughts or the external stream of events which inexorably carries us along on its rapidly moving current.

We should by no means overlook the significant and hopeful advances of recent decades in the intellectual as in other fields. One of the most promising tendencies of our world is the way in which we have been freeing ourselves from outdated and limited patterns, in the intellectual sphere no less than in our political and social life. If anything, the balance has swung too far in the other direction. Far from regarding our heritage of attitudes and customs as above question or subject only to limited and slow modifications, as in the earlier civilizations, we tend to look upon it as something we can change or abolish almost at will.

The basis of this critical re-examination of the roots of human society has been a renewed recognition of the emotional and spiritual nature of man, something that was taken for granted in all the earlier civilizations but was virtually lost sight of in the long desert interval of Victorian materialism. The rediscovery of the emotional roots of man's nature through the work of Freud, Jung, Adler, and their successors has, in fact, "caught on" to such an extent that we are in constant danger of substituting mere psychological techniques and practices for the genuine new synthesis society needs. Far from having achieved a balanced appreciation of the emotional and spiritual requirements of man in contemporary society, we have become an easy prey to fashionable aberrations that conceal rather than reveal the deep-rooted problems involved. But the mere fact that we are at least beginning to recognize the importance of these emotional forces is a great step forward as compared with the situation of a hundred or even fifty years ago. The present direction of our thinking holds out hope that we may yet succeed in finding a way to integrate and give expression to our emotional and spiritual energies in the still fluid patterns of industrial mass societies.

All this is unquestionably to the good. What has thus far been conspicuously lacking is the over-all view, the integrating vision that will enable us to re-establish our control over these unruly cultural floods and to reintegrate the varied traditions of contemporary man into a new and comprehensive pattern. From decade to decade, almost from year to year, this central task has become more urgent. It encounters us at virtually every level of existence. We meet it in the cleavage between the fundamental religious impulses and traditions and the increasingly vigorous secular trends of the Western world. We are faced with the same task throughout our political, economic, and social existence, in the need to keep our varied activities from drawing too far apart or blindly colliding with one another. It confronts us in another guise in our efforts to maintain some measure of balance between the claims of public and private affairs, between central control and local initiative. It is most formidably present in the vital field of defense and national security, particularly in the effort to maintain an over-all strategic control over the bewildering multiplicity of new weapons, armament systems, and totally new forms of warfare.

This proliferation of new forces, and the intellectual disorganization that accompanies it, have nowhere been more clearly evident than in the central organ of all cultural integration, the field of education. The essential functions of education which were recognized and acknowledged by all past societies have been so largely lost to sight that it now requires a certain effort even to recall them to the modern imagination. For education in its origins was unequivocally regarded as a matter of public rather than private significance. Its purpose was not to foster individual excellence or to teach a combination of assorted knowledge and skills, but to initiate each new generation into the values and traditions of the community and train it for the carrying on of this established tradition and way of life.

Within the past half-century, most of the elements in this millennial educational tradition have either broken down or been severely weakened. In Western society, at least, education has tended to withdraw more and more completely from its original public function in order to concentrate on inculcating knowledge and developing skills for the advancement of the individual. The inevitable result has been a loss of direction and coherence throughout the educational process. In ceasing to aim at the transmission of an integrated culture, traditional or scientific, education has tended more and more to disintegrate into the teaching of uncorrelated conglomerates of the most diverse kinds of information.

Perhaps the most striking illustration of our lack of integration with the past has been the increasing neglect and erosion in that field of studies which until our own age constituted the strongest cultural bond in Western civilization—the classical studies of Greek and Roman antiquity. As recently as a generation ago, the classics still occupied a dominant place in the Western educational system, particularly in higher education. The study of Latin and Greek was the acknowledged medium for gaining an understanding of the roots of society. Latin, in particular, had for more than two thousand years represented not only the universal language of the West but a universal discipline of thought. The structure of the Latin language, with its complex rolling sentences, its sense of balance among the grammatical elements, and its meticulous expression of the relationships between them, had been of immeasurable assistance to Western man in learning to face complex situations and "lay out" their various factors in clearly articulated surveys that could be taken in at a glance.

Latin has been the school not merely of fastidious scholars and pettifogging lawyers but of statesmen and generals and merchant princes. It taught them to see not only the facts of a problem but their multiform relations to each other and to other facts, to think habitually in terms of situations and structural patterns. Classical studies today are too often derided as an expression of mere social snobbery or, at best, a precious cult of refined scholarship. In reality, their decline from a living source of inspiration to a vanishing academic curiosity is symptomatic of the radical change that has occurred in the whole structure of Western thought. It neatly symbolizes the general weakening in man's determination to keep a grasp on the world he is creating and to retain control over the forces he has unleashed.

In the place of the traditional classical education, we now have an increasing emphasis on training in the sciences. And, as C. P. Snow has pointed out in his famous discussion of *The Two Cultures and the Scientific Revolution,* with the rise of the sciences to a position of equality and even predominance over the classics our educational system has been rent by a growing division and lack of communication between scientists and scholars trained in the literary tradition. Other illustrations of the disorganization that besets our educational system and our intellectual life could be multiplied indefinitely. The study of history could and should be playing a more vital role than at any time in the past. With the global expansion of our range of vision and the accelerated tempo of our lives, a branch of knowledge that was formerly a matter of aristocratic leisure, a luxury, has become an elementary requirement of responsible citizenship. Yet the recognition, to say nothing of the implementation, of this vital function has hardly begun.

Science, the magic key to our well-being and progress, now stands unchallenged in the center of public interest. Yet even among the scientists, very few have yet shown an awareness of the quite peculiar and difficult problems of continued integration which their own discipline presents and upon which its progress ultimately depends. The field of science has become so vast and highly specialized that despite the practical advantages it enjoys, it quite literally threatens to fall apart, in an intellectual if not in a material sense. Few scientists are any longer capable of maintaining a comprehensive view of their own fields; far fewer have succeeded in retaining any idea of science as a whole.

The practical effects of this general lack of orientation reveal themselves in innumerable ways. We are experiencing an ever-increasing difficulty in maintaining public and private affairs and interests in their proper balance. Our failing sense of direction appears plainly in the endless debates on public matters—endless not merely because of the complexity of the subject matter, but because of our increasing tendency to argue without first ascertaining exactly what we are arguing about. On a larger scale, the effects are equally evident in the difficulties experienced by the Western world as a whole in finding a common ground both for discussion within its own ranks and for the necessary debates with the two other great cultural groups of our contemporary world, the Communist camp and the resurgent nations of Asia and Africa. Perhaps the supreme example of our present-day intellectual disorganization is to be found in our strangely inconsistent attitudes toward the critical issues of war and peace.

5

Power in War and Peace

THERE CAN BE no dispute with the oft-repeated assertion that the maintenance of peace is the
overriding problem of our time. Little as its
consequences can be foreseen in detail, the release of power in a
conflict among major powers under contemporary conditions
would clearly be so overwhelming in its destructive force that
almost no price would seem excessive if it could ensure the avoid-
ance of such a catastrophe.

Men differ, therefore, not on the goal to be sought but on the
means to be employed and the nature of the dangers to be overcome. Too often, in the years since the Second World War,
attention has been one-sidedly focused on the problem of the
control of nuclear weapons, which, although undoubtedly the
most dramatic, are by no means the only symptom of mankind's
present peril. In reality, the present dependence on nuclear
weapons represents only the culmination of the much wider process that we have described as the general expansion of power in
industrial society. Having observed this process as it developed in
the civilian sphere, we are in a better position to examine the
composition and changing significance of power in military affairs
and in the relations among states.

The Evolution of War and Peace

As they developed their power through the ages, men have inevitably been drawn into closer and closer relations with one another. Beginning in prehistoric times, the separate groups scattered over the globe have continually met, clashed, and either exterminated each other or gradually fused into larger units— tribes, peoples, nations, civilizations. In this long process, it is natural that men have been intensively concerned not only with their own power but with that of their neighbors as well. In their pursuit of a larger freedom within their own natural environment, they have also been forced to try to develop the means of avoiding conquest and enslavement or worse at the hands of their neighbors. This basic sense of mistrust and rivalry between human groups has acted right down to the present as a powerful spur to the development of more and more strength, to the accumulation of more and more power, and hence to man's conquest of a wider and wider sphere of autonomous action within nature.

To appreciate the full significance of these intergroup rivalries in the genesis of our contemporary power problems, we must go all the way back to the primitive groups of the roving and hunting period. To its members, the horde offered the priceless advantages of physical and psychological support, the solidarity and assistance that man in his weakness imperatively needed in order to survive. Above all, it offered him that most precious of all supports, a sense of belonging. Every member had his niche in a complex hierarchy determined by age, blood relationship, and personal traits of strength, assertiveness, cunning, and so forth. Each man stood shoulder to shoulder within the closed circle of his kinsmen.

This intense spirit of kinship persisted deep into the agricultural phase of man's development. Just as the nomadic tribes, under the harsh conditions of the desert, could maintain peace and solidarity only through an inexorable application of the complementary laws of hospitality and blood vengeance, so we frequently find in the Nordic sagas the shield wall of kinsmen likened to the stakes of a fence, all of which are linked and bound together. If one of the group was injured or broken down, all suffered alike, perhaps fatally. The peace of the kin group, the complete suppression of violence within it, became the central social concern to which every other commitment, every consideration of individual self-interest, even the upholding of the individual's dignity, was ruthlessly subordinated.

Between different hordes and tribes, on the other hand, there was for a very long time no sense of familiarity or common interest at all. Meeting by chance on the steppes or in the forests and jungles, such primitive groups could experience no feeling of kinship but only a sense of utter strangeness and unfamiliarity, a complete absence of any emotional or rational community of interest such as might have served as a basis for confidence or even predictability. "Other man," in so far as he was recognized at all as a fellow being made in a common image, was for primitive man essentially a stranger, uncanny and by no means to be trusted.

Under such circumstances, the relations between different groups could not be governed by custom and unwritten law as they were within the horde itself. In any meeting between alien tribes, there was no way for either of them to know what the other was likely to do. Inevitably, their contacts were based upon mutual estimates not so much of "intentions" as of "capabilities." The relations between them tended to be purely relations of power, the respective measure of power each group appeared capable of exerting. The result was to channel the contacts between alien groups directly into the forms of a power rivalry—not because their wills necessarily clashed, but because, whether they clashed or not, their mutual fears drove them to suspicion and hence to action against each other.

It was only with the transition to agriculture and settlement that this pattern of relations based exclusively on power began to be gradually modified. Settlement—or, with the nomadic tribes, the gradual staking out of regular grazing grounds—meant both consolidation and an increase in assured supplies of grains and animal foods. This in turn led to a corresponding increase in population as the roving hordes settled down in villages and expanded into tribes. Tribes gradually expanded, by fusion or conquest, into larger areas and societies, into kingdoms and empires. Higher and higher forms of political organization became necessary, from the "old man" of the horde to the village headman or council of elders, the tribal chieftain or district leader, finally the kingly or imperial despot.

At the same time, the experience of settlement laid the basis for a gradual transformation in the relations between different groups and peoples. Tribes that were becoming settled in the same general area were virtually forced to accept a measure of mutual coexistence, even though only by a sort of tacit consent. Gradually, and with innumerable relapses into primitive savagery, the earlier attitude of complete "alienness" must have given way to a growing sense of familiarity. While it did not remotely approach the close familiarity existing *within* the tribe, it made possible a state of mutual toleration that could eventually develop into a degree of mutual confidence.

In due course this profound change of attitude was bound to result in the attempt to establish some kind of definite institutional relationship. Unlike the accidental meetings between roving hordes, the relations of permanently settled neighbors demanded a measure of formalization and consolidation. At the outset, however, this institutional pattern tended to be anything but a pacific one. Since the interchanges between different communities were still basically concerned with power, the establishment of permanent relationships necessarily started from war rather than peace. In war, their fundamental sense of "unrelatedness" simply crystallized into a definite cultural state. The crystallization of a recognizable state of peace, on the other hand, would have required the bridging of this gulf of alienness and the establishment of some common ground of mutual recognition and trust. Only gradually was a state of explicit tolerance and good will—a state of peace—developed as the result of increasing contacts, a growing exchange of goods, and above all by specific treaties determining definite spheres of interest.

This progression from the primitive state of alienness to a consolidated state of either war or peace is, of course, a most difficult process to follow or document. We find far more accounts of conflicts than of peaceful relations in the records that have come down to us. Even when there is evidence of a state of formal peace, we usually do not know how it was established or how far it extended. Until well into our modern age we have only tantalizing glimpses of the periods of peaceful coexistence that must undoubtedly have occurred between episodes of conflict.

The earliest of these glimpses is afforded by the state system that was established about the middle of the second millennium B.C. along the eastern shores of the Mediterranean. Around 1800 B.C. a wave of migrant peoples from the north swept over this whole area, overwhelming all resistance with their new war chariots. In the wake of this invasion the older peoples of Egypt, Crete, and Babylonia combined with the new states established by the invaders—Achaia in Greece, the Hittite Empire in Asia Minor, the Mitanni Empire in northern Syria—to form a state system that was characterized by a remarkable coherence in spite of wide differences of race, culture, and language. From the records that have been pieced together, we can see this state system emerging out of the preceding darkness and confusion in a surprisingly advanced and well-developed form. We find not only extensive diplomatic exchanges but a clear demarcation between the great powers and the states of lesser rank, with dynastic intermarriages and even mutual guarantees of dynastic solidarity. Among the surviving documents are treaties establishing peace as well as carefully formulated compacts of mutual friendship and cooperation.

The same pattern of coexistence is characteristic of a series of similar systems in the East: the Hellenistic kingdoms and the

Islamic, Indian, Chinese, and Indonesian state systems. Here, too, we find a number of large or small states developing an elaborate system of etiquette to govern their relations and constant rivalries and intrigues. As yet, however, we do not find any clear-cut institutional system comprehending both war and peace. For this development we must turn to the evolution of Western civilization.

The era of Western development that begins with the rise of Greece and Rome was more than just a continuation of the earlier Egyptian and Mesopotamian civilizations. Entering the Mediterranean world as primitive but highly gifted tribes, the Greeks and Romans gradually absorbed many of the cultural achievements of the older civilizations, their myths and artistic inspirations, their scientific concepts and early attainments in mathematics, astronomy, and medicine. But the Greeks and the Romans did not adopt what had become the standard ideas about the relations between different peoples. Instead of taking over and continuing the elaborate system of the ancient Near East, they started all over again along entirely original lines.

The Greeks offer a particularly striking illustration of the obstacles with which any idea of a peaceful coexistence had to contend. As we first encounter them at the beginning of the first millennium B.C., the Greeks were strongly united in their common civilization and radically divided in their political allegiances. They revered the same gods, assembled at the same sanctuaries for the great religious festivals and games, and spoke a common language, though in different dialects. They felt proud to belong to a particular stock, the Hellenes, characterized by common traits that sharply distinguished them both from the barbaric tribes of the north and from the Oriental peoples. Yet despite this profound sense of cultural community, the Greeks remained sharply divided in their separate urban political groupings. The sense of solidarity and familiarity that was such a strongly marked characteristic of the Greek city-states abruptly broke off beyond their limits. Between different cities, especially between near neighbors, there was a feeling of alienness and a spirit of rivalry that still recalled the attitude of the most primitive human groups.

So acute was this sense of universal rivalry that a state of perpetual hostility, which could at any moment explode into open war, appeared to the Greek mind as the natural way of life. Peace, to the Greeks, was not a normal state of affairs. It was an exceptional condition that had to be formally established by special treaties—and not, moreover, as a permanent consolidation of relations, but only for limited periods of, say, thirty or fifty years. In consequence, the Greeks were never able to achieve any kind of stable political unity. Even in the struggle against the Persians, when the feeling of cultural solidarity was at its height, many cities joined forces with the invader. While both Sparta and Athens made the attempt to group a number of cities under their leadership, in the long run they each failed to hold them together. Undeterred by their common cultural bonds or even by considerations of common prudence, the Greeks continued their intercity conflicts until, exhausted by this continuous bloodletting, they finally relapsed into a coma under foreign domination.

In contrast to the reckless individualism of the Greeks, the Romans were nothing if not sober and staid. Their deep sense of social stability led them to base their relations with other peoples on the idea of a natural state of coexistence rather than of enmity. While the Greeks most clearly reflected the sense of alienness between different communities, the Romans just as unmistakably felt themselves to exist within a network of implied or explicit bonds. Any form of contact with other cities, however slight, was considered as constituting *amicitia,* or friendly relations. Even war was regarded by the Romans not so much as a means for extirpating their opponents as for coercing them into a stable and, for the most part, not intolerable relationship.

Within such a socially determined world, war was not the glorious adventure that irresistibly attracted the Greeks. It was a very grave matter, one that concerned the order established by the gods themselves and therefore had to be acceptable to the gods as well as to men. To the Romans, war was not a natural state but had to arise out of a just cause, a prior infraction by the enemy of Rome's own rights or those of her allies. It is true that to reconcile their lofty aspirations with their somewhat opportunistic practice, the Romans had often enough to go to extreme lengths in order to put their enemies "in the wrong before the gods." Yet the mere fact that they were so seriously concerned about this necessity shows that their constant emphasis upon the orderly character of their relations with other peoples was something more than mere legalism or hypocrisy.

Thus the Romans tended to regard the spectacular advance of their own power, from the city on the Tiber across the whole Mediterranean basin and into northern and central Europe, not as a series of unprincipled conquests but as a process of "pacification." They thought of this process as an extension of the stability and legal orderliness of their own life—the *Pax Romana*—over as much of the world as they could reach.

In St. Augustine's *City of God,* this secular tradition of the *Pax Romana* was taken over and blended with the manifold aspects of the Biblical concept of peace—peace of the soul with God, peace between spirit and flesh, peace as the reign of justice between man and man. At the apex of antiquity, Augustine's vision of peace, embracing within its magnificent sweep all of the religious and profane implications of peace, became the beacon that was to illumine the path of Western civilization in the dark and turbulent ages that followed.

With the breakdown of the Roman Empire amid the incursions of the Germanic and Slavic tribes, the Roman and Biblical notions of war and peace clashed with the primitive but tenacious attachment of the barbarian invaders to their own ideas of personal rule and of a sacred order of rights that stemmed directly from tribal experience. The highly developed institutional structure of the Roman Empire gave way to a diffuse conglomeration of ill-defined personal hierarchies in the "feudal system" that for almost a thousand years became the dominant pattern of state and society. But in breaking up the political organization of the Roman Empire and replacing it with their own looser system, these Germanic and Slavic tribes also injected a new and positive element into the complex medieval synthesis. Where the Roman word *pax* had suggested merely a cessation of strife and conflict, a laying down of arms, the word that the Germanic peoples use for peace, *Friede,* goes far beyond this connotation. It means not merely a passive cessation of strife, but the introduction of a positive force making for peace, of positive action to bring contending parties into a friendly state of mind in their relations to each other.

As a result of these divergent influences, medieval Western civilization in its attitude toward war and peace reveals the same inadequately reconciled contradictions that we have observed in its general outlook. On the one side, there was the splintering up of public authority into a multitude of separate "rights," both of individuals and of such corporate bodies as the estates of a territory, the citizens of a town, the members of a guild, an ecclesiastical chapter, or a university. All these different rights stood side by side, jostled each other, conflicted with each other. At the same time the confusion was tempered by a deep-rooted and almost universal bias in favor of peaceful and harmonious relations, as an ideal if not as a practical rule of conduct.

The embodiment of this spirit of peacefulness and good will was the medieval king. To the medieval peoples the king was far more than a mere *de facto* ruler. He was the executant of a divine mission whose highest responsibility was precisely that of resolving strife and imposing what was known as "the king's peace." Though he ruled by a divine right that even the greatest reverses could not entirely extinguish, his right to kingship was conditioned by, and dependent upon, the means to make it effective. To discharge his primary obligation of maintaining peace and assuring justice, the king required the power of the sword. A ruler who failed in this obligation, who proved incapable of protecting the rights of his people and defending them against aggressors, could be judged to have forfeited his office. It is true that such standards were seldom rigorously enforced. Here, as in other spheres, the people of the Middle Ages preferred to let a radical contradiction rest rather than try to resolve it by pushing it to its ultimate conclusions.

BALANCE OF POWER AND RULE OF LAW

As modern Western civilization begins to emerge from the matrix of medieval Christendom, we recognize yet another great stage in the evolution of man's use of power. Its outstanding feature was the breakup of the religious system that had served as an integrating force in the medieval world and its virtual dethronement by a group of vigorous national states, established on an out-and-out secular basis, which were now destined to become the key elements of modern Western civilization much as the Greek cities had been some two thousand years earlier. First Spain, France, England, and the Hapsburg dominions, and then the Netherlands, Sweden, Russia, Prussia, and Italy successively entered upon the European scene as clearly defined political units. Although the new states of Europe inherited from the Middle Ages a strong sense of community and a full awareness of their similar religious and political foundations, this underlying sense of kinship did not prevent their clashing with each other far more frequently and violently than in the past. As their forces increasingly turned outward, they involved themselves in a perpetual and ever-sharper conflict of interests and ambitions. At first these clashes involved only certain limited groups of states in the western, northern, and other parts of Europe. In the course of time, the separate areas of political interaction and conflict began to interlock until finally the struggle with Napoleonic France fused all Europe from the Atlantic to the Urals into a single political system.

The European state system that thus emerged from the diffuse political organization of the Middle Ages was the first developed political community in history to be based almost exclusively upon the power relations among its members. A continuous and all-embracing power rivalry provided the common framework within which the individual states awoke to consciousness and developed as consolidated units. As the medieval sense of community grew weaker and the passions of the religious struggle began to wane, their relations came to be more and more completely determined by the power rivalry itself. With the increasingly close intertwining of their individual interests, the formerly intermittent relations between the different members of the European community coalesced into a continuous state of rivalry that enveloped all its members at all times.

Precisely because the struggle for power had thus become both universal and perpetual, the individual rivalries of the different members formed a structure in which they tended to balance one another. Within the general power competition they were held together by definite patterns of antagonism and alignment that persisted through generations, notably in the rivalry between France and the House of Hapsburg and the parallel antagonism that pitted England against France and Spain. Prompted by their own interests and ambitions, such powers as the Netherlands, Turkey, Sweden, Prussia, and Russia joined in these alignments and helped to maintain a rough over-all balance of power that sometimes embraced a number of independent but interlocking local balances of power.

In the century and a half between the end of the wars of religion in 1648 and the beginning of the wars of the French Revolution in 1792, the European community came closer to a perfect system of political mechanics than any other state system before or after. The power of the individual states had by this time been developed to a point where it could be effectively mobilized and maintained through relatively prolonged conflicts. At the same time, a number of factors served to limit the intensity and scale of these conflicts and to stabilize the whole procedure within mutually acceptable bounds. The strength of the key members, the great powers, was evenly matched. The land powers were balanced by the sea powers. The checkerboard locations of the member states made it easy for two states to join forces against an opponent situated between them—and for that opponent, in turn, to invoke the aid of other powers lying beyond its assailants. The conflicts themselves were generally of limited scope, and tended to center around certain key border areas such as Flanders and northern Italy. Because of the relatively small size of the areas and the simplicity of the forces involved, the risks were limited and calculable with a high degree of accuracy. Finally, the power to wage war on this limited basis lay in the hands of a very few men who were able to use it in quite cold-blooded maneuvers and counter-maneuvers with little interference by public opinion or other influences.

The classical doctrine of the balance of power as a dynamism of objective forces and necessities had an exact parallel in the theory of a natural balance of forces that was simultaneously developed in the field of natural science. Just as Newton succeeded in tracing the order and harmony of the celestial constellations back to the balance of the gravitational forces operating between the elements of the solar system, so the exponents of the balance of power strove, in the same spirit and with analogous concepts, to grasp the nature of the conflicting forces and national interests in the political constellation of Europe in such a way as to achieve a balance between them and thus assure order and harmony in the European state system.

It would be a mistake to regard the power politics of that time as primarily an expression of aggressiveness, greed, or ambition, prominently as all these motives did come into play. In a more fundamental sense, its motive force was the state of uncertainty and apprehension that continued to prevail among the members of the European state system just as they had among more primitive human groups. In a system determined exclusively by considerations of power, states and statesmen are prone to resort to hostile action precisely because they fear the consequences of *not* acting, and of thus failing to forestall a possible hostile move by their rivals. This compulsion to preventive action in its turn creates new causes for mutual apprehension and leads to further actions by other parties.

This fundamental weakness was one of the reasons why the balance-of-power system did not work out in practice with anything like the accuracy attributed to it in theory. Shifts in power between the different states were often too slowly recognized to be effectively dealt with. Yet even though the system responded in practice far more sluggishly than it was supposed to, it nevertheless assured for centuries a fundamental equilibrium within the European community as a whole, and with it the continuing existence of nearly all its members. At its height, in William III's efforts to arouse Europe against the growing power and ambitions of Louis XIV, the balance of power had something of a heroic note, a clarion call to stand together for the common defense. It was only as the original impulse subsided and the system degenerated into a routine method that its fundamental drabness made itself felt, until by the end of the eighteenth century it could lead to the cynical division of hapless Poland by its three rapacious neighbors.

As the members of the European state system pursued the intricate movements of their common power rivalry, a wholly different concept of the relations between nations had been slowly emerging as a by-product of the development of the constitutional state in England and the Netherlands. It was but natural that the establishment of a rule of law as a guarantee of peaceful coexistence *within* the state should have led to an endeavor to extend the same principle into the area of relations *between* states. The rule of law within the state, it seemed, would be complete only when the state, too, was subject to law in its relationships with other states.

This tendency to think in terms of a relationship based upon law rather than on a precarious balance of power received support from a wide variety of sources. One of these was the Christian tradition; a second was the philosophical outlook of the Enlightenment, to which war appeared as nothing but a barbarous stupidity. Still a third factor was the steadily increasing development of economic ties among the nations, brought about as the direct result of spontaneous private actions by individuals who were availing themselves of the new opportunities opened up by the recognition of a "private sphere" exempt from state interference. The development of a world-wide system of private economic bonds, it seemed, should tend to hold down the divisive power rivalry between the states and unite the peoples into a global community which, while economic and private in character, would nevertheless assume a political and public character through its effect upon the maintenance of world peace.

For several decades in the middle of the nineteenth century it seemed that the development of the modern state system was actually proceeding along these evolutionary and relatively peaceful lines. Conflicts among the European powers were infrequent and brief, had relatively little impact on civilian life, and seemed on the whole to be going out of fashion as the powers resorted with increasing frequency to international conferences as a more humane and civilized method of effecting such adjustments in the balance of power as changing circumstances required. The predominance of a single group of great powers served to keep the world as a whole at peace and to make possible the undisturbed expansion of the world economy while the overseas territories were being progressively divided up into European zones of interest and spheres of influence.

At the same time, international trade was undergoing a tremendous expansion under the twin impulses of the industrial revolution and the opening up of areas hitherto closed to Western commerce. Industry and trade, unlike territorial possessions, did not constitute a fixed quantity but represented an expanding potential in which it seemed that everybody could share and in which cooperation in accordance with the new policy of free trade might prove mutually beneficial. This discovery transformed society for several decades into something that came remarkably close to the dream of an economic community of mankind, a universal "private sphere" in which the political divisions represented by the states seemed destined to retain little more than administrative significance.

This sense of a progressive evolution in international affairs retained a large measure of verisimilitude until some time after 1871. Thereafter, it began to be increasingly overshadowed by the resumption of more acute forms of power rivalry. At bottom, the international order still reflected not so much the outlook of the new industrial classes as the persistence of the feudal-anarchic spirit that found its characteristic expression in the traditional sovereign right of states to go to war with one another as their interests appeared to dictate. What was really new in the situation was the increasingly bellicose trend of popular opinion, whipped up by the new mass media with a facility that clearly reflected the lack of legitimate emotional outlets in the new industrial civilization. Thus the initial breakthrough of the new industrial forces in the so-called "age of imperialism" at the end of the nineteenth century was marked by a series of violent outbursts of mass hysteria that formed an ominous prelude to the four-year emotional orgy of the First World War.

THE TRANSFORMATION OF MILITARY POWER

Throughout this long period the forms and characteristics of military power had remained remarkably simple and consistent. From prehistoric times until well into the nineteenth century, the basis of military power was simply the fighting man together with the land that fed him. Thucydides and Machiavelli, writing almost two thousand years apart, drew attention to this elementary fact in almost identical terms. Throughout the long initial period in which men roamed the forests and plains, moving here and there in response to the variations in climate and food supply, power rested entirely in the individual horde and the strength and enterprise of its members. Its application was concentrated and instantaneous; if two groups of primitive men met and clashed, the issue was generally decided on the spot. More stable conditions first began to develop with the change to agriculture and settlement, which resulted in a much closer dependence of the human group upon the land which sustained its existence. For more than seven thousand years, from the earliest agricultural settlements in the Near East to the eve of the First World War, land, as the primary source of nourishment and hence of the men who could be raised for fighting, became the basis of power both within the community itself and in its struggles with other communities.

This dependence of power upon the land had historical consequences of far-reaching significance. Originally concentrated in the individual horde or tribe, power now became much more widely diffused. With the primitive means of administration and transportation available, it could not easily be mobilized or centrally controlled. It tended rather to be parceled out among a number of landowning families, held together by a loose system of tribal or feudal allegiances or, more rarely, as in the great Oriental civilizations, by a bureaucracy closely connected with the large landowners. From time to time, men of exceptional energy might arise and fuse these territorial cells into powerful kingdoms or empires. But the difficulties of controlling vast and poorly organized areas of land always proved insurmountable in the long run. Systems of control would last for a few generations, then break down again. Power would fall back from the hands of the central government or dynasty into those of the local landowning families until finally the empire or kingdom disintegrated.

The dependence of power mainly upon the land affected not only the internal structure of the community but also the possibility of projecting its strength outward. Agricultural manpower is tied down to its productive tasks and is difficult to mobilize. The loose territorial organizations of the pre-industrial age could mobilize only a fraction of their total populations, primarily those groups which had made warfare their hereditary avocation as feudal aristocracies or warrior castes. Cities were generally much better able to organize their full strength, but only for short campaigns in their immediate neighborhood. Otherwise they had to employ mercenaries, who were liable to quit the fight as soon as the funds gave out. It was only within the past few centuries that the modern states of Europe developed the means of organizing and mobilizing a substantial part of their manpower for an indefinite period.

Another basic limitation on the deployment of military power arose from the difficulties of supply. The limited means of transport available in agricultural civilizations sharply restricted the forces that could be sent into the field and maintained there. Throughout most of this period we find not only the same basic types of military forces—the foot soldier or the horseman, the oardriven vessel or the sailing ship—but a remarkable constancy in the numbers involved. In the rare instances when a despotic land-based power attempted to surmount these natural limitations, the concentration of overly large masses created embarrassment rather than the overwhelming strength intended. The sheer size and unmanageability of such forces frequently led to rout and disaster. It was not until late in the nineteenth century that the progress of the industrial revolution produced the technical means for mobilizing, transporting, and supplying mass armies.

Such limitations created a serious vulnerability to the use of more concentrated and mobile forms of power. For centuries the sedentary agricultural civilizations of the Near East, Western Europe, India, and China were subject to attack by waves of nomadic peoples surging forth from two great centers, the Arabian desert and the great Eurasian steppe. Compared with the settled peoples, these migratory tribes had the twofold advantage of concentrated manpower and superior mobility. Although greatly inferior in numbers, they were able to harass and frequently to conquer the sedentary populations. From the earliest dawn of history down to the conquest of China by the Manchus in the seventeenth century, this conflict between the settler and the nomad was a central theme in the history of military power.

Somewhat similar was the role of sea power. Like the mounted hordes of nomads, naval fleets enjoyed the advantages of sharply centralized strength and superior mobility in relation to the diffuse forces of land powers. To this was added the advantage of a safe line of retreat. Naval forces could swoop down on the enemy coastline at any point and could generally count upon getting away again before the defenders could rally their forces. Thus the seafaring nations, like the nomadic peoples, often exercised an influence quite out of proportion to their manpower and intrinsic strength. The control established by the nations of Europe over the other continents, particularly the great Oriental land empires, was won and exercised by remarkably small forces, consisting of no more than a few naval squadrons and a few thousands or tens of thousands of troops under bold and resourceful leadership.

By the outbreak of the First World War, the progress of the industrial revolution had virtually brought to an end this prolonged period in which the development of power had been based primarily upon agricultural settlement and the fighting men it nurtured. This shift, however, was an exceedingly gradual process. The pre-industrial types of land and sea warfare had reached their supreme expression in the wars of the French Revolution and Napoleon, which crystallized the forms of organization and strategic direction of forces in a manner that continued to dominate the thinking of military leaders throughout the nineteenth century. The effects of the industrial revolution, in contrast, for a long time remained largely restricted to the civilian sector of society. Though willing to make use of the new technical devices provided by the progress of industrial development, the military leaders of the nineteenth century were not prepared to revise the basic rules of warfare to which they had become wedded.

One innovation that did find general acceptance was the total mobilization of manpower. The *levée en masse* inaugurated by the revolutionary French Republic had been promptly adopted by France's opponents and in the course of the nineteenth century came to be the generally accepted principle, even though the shortness of most wars restricted its application in practice. At the same time, the problem of maintaining these enlarged forces was met by greatly improved methods of transportation and supply, made possible by the growing material resources of the belligerent countries. The size of the belligerent forces, which for thousands of years had remained at a remarkably low level, began to rise substantially, though still not in proportion to the increase in general population. Effective control of these massed forces was made possible by the clarification of strategic principles that had occurred in the Napoleonic era and the development of modern, highly centralized general staff organizations.

On the other hand, the vast concentrations of mechanical and chemical energy and scientific knowledge that were already being built up by the industrial revolution at first remained largely un-exploited for military purposes. The most significant of the modern innovations introduced between 1859 and 1871—the use of the telegraph and of railroads in the mass deployment and direction of land forces—were grafted, by and large, onto the strategic concepts derived from Napoleon's campaigns. At sea, the impact of the industrial revolution was somewhat greater. The successive introduction of the steamship, the iron hull, and finally the iron-clad ship threw naval warfare into a period of confusion around the middle of the century. But these innovations affected naval tactics, not strategy, which by the end of the century had reverted to its traditional forms and was still being reformulated and systematized by Admiral Mahan and Sir Julian Corbett on the basis of the records of the old wars.

All but unobserved during these seemingly indecisive decades was the quiet yet immensely significant change that was taking place in the basic sources of power and in the accompanying forms of national leadership. So long as power had remained predominantly based upon the land and concentrated mainly in the hands of the great families, its exercise had remained intimately linked with the discharge of public responsibilities. The landed classes had served both as the natural local authorities and, to a large extent, as the public authority of their countries in both military and civil matters.

The new forms of power brought into being by the industrial revolution bore a quite different relationship to the society within which they developed. Even more than in their technical aspects, these new forms of power differed from what had preceded them by reason of their essentially "private" character. Created as the result of private endeavor, they were manipulated and directed not in accordance with any public necessity but in accordance with the established criteria of the "private sphere." Though industrial leadership was becoming no less a source of power than hereditary landownership, its influence, unlike that of the landed aristocracy, remained almost exclusively of a private nature. It was directed toward production, not toward the exercise of either military or political responsibilities. The earlier unity of leadership functions in the hands of the landowning aristocracy increasingly tended to break down amid the infinitely greater complexity of the social organization created by the industrial revolution.

The first 150 years of the industrial revolution thus witnessed a growing discrepancy within the structure of Western civilization. The political and military framework was still determined by the old forms of power. Within this traditional framework, new forms and forces were taking shape that had failed as yet to gain any significant influence in reshaping the old patterns. The result was a growing tension between a pattern of power and life that had outlived itself and a set of completely new forces to which it afforded wholly insufficient scope. The event that finally shattered this obsolete pattern, in military as in political affairs, was the outbreak of the First World War and the liberation of a whole series of pent-up forces which were to revolutionize not only the character of that conflict but the whole of human existence.

THE PARADOX OF TOTAL WAR

The experience of the two World Wars affected the conditions of war and peace in a manner no less far-reaching than their revo-

lutionary impact on the life of society generally. These two conflicts brought to a final close the transformation in the art of war
that had been initiated in the earlier stages of the industrial revolution. For the industrialized countries, at least, the long epoch of
power resting upon land and men reached its end. In its place was
inaugurated a new epoch in which the bases of the new industrial
civilization—mass organization, industrial skill, and scientific imagination—became the main sources of a much more complex system of power, a system in which military power as such represented
only one element.

The four years of the First World War sufficed to implement
the decisive shift of military power from its previous agricultural
base. The enormous latent power of industrial civilization was
abruptly diverted from the peaceful purposes for which it had
been developed—still in an improvised and primitive fashion in
the 1914–18 war, but in a much more systematic manner in the
Second World War.

Where military power up to 1914 had remained sharply separated from all the other forms of power, warfare since that date
has drawn more and more widely and systematically upon the
whole range of our expanding industrial civilization. Novel scientific and technical means have been applied not only to the
elaboration of the traditional methods and weapons of warfare
but to their extension into new spheres of operations, as in submarine and air warfare, not to mention the development of such
wholly new, essentially scientific conceptions as radar, missiles,
and nuclear weapons. Many of the arts of peace have been similarly diverted to military uses: medicine, to biological warfare;
the chemical industries, to chemical warfare; advertising and
depth psychology, to propaganda and "psychological warfare." As
one scientific discovery has led to another, the means of waging
war have almost automatically extended and diversified themselves. The atomic bomb was followed, as an almost inescapable
consequence, by the development of the hydrogen bomb and of
tactical nuclear weapons.

This change in the sources of military power raised wider problems than could be appreciated in the heat of conflict. The shift from power based upon land to power based upon industrial and scientific resources was more than simply a shift from one source of strength to another, from a lower to a higher gear. It was a change-over from a system that, with all its limitations, had been fundamentally in harmony with the exigencies of military conflict to one that in many respects was at odds with the nature of war itself.

In its simplicity and ruggedness, the system of power based upon land and men had been thoroughly in accord with military requirements. There was a natural harmony between the aristocratic social system and the military system that grew out of it. The social hierarchy and its ideology were equally warlike. The local landowner could easily transform himself into a military leader. The economic basis was still so limited, equipment was developed at so slow a pace, that the sinews of war could be stockpiled in advance of a conflict. The fabric of life, being simple and flexible, was well adapted to war. The transition from peace to war occasioned no major dislocation of the economic and social structure. The latter could be disrupted, crops destroyed, trees hacked down, buildings burned or blown up, yet this damage was rarely crippling or lasting.

The shift to a predominantly industrial and scientific power base, on the other hand, involved the reorientation of a system that was fundamentally geared not to military but to peacetime requirements. The new industrial system differed from its predecessor in almost every respect. It was certainly not devoid of the passion for power and prestige. In its own way it reflected an unprecedented outburst of such passion. But it had generally sought this power not in the political but in the private sphere; not through military conquest but through the "conquest of nature" and through economic production. Contrary to the assertions of Lenin and other latter-day Marxists, its basic impulses had not been directed toward war, nor did its essential interests depend upon war. On the contrary, it was based upon economic specialization and depended for its undisturbed progress upon conditions of peace, freedom of exchange between countries, safety of capital invested abroad, and so on.

Where the industrial civilization is open to legitimate criticism is not in any overemphasis on military power but, on the contrary, in its tendency to *underrate* the significance of military strength as the basic framework that alone enabled it to attain its present pre-eminence. The development of this blind spot in the outlook of industrial civilization was furthered by the peculiar nature of the deterrent force that throughout the nineteenth century did most to maintain the peaceful atmosphere in which capitalism could flourish. This was the British Navy, whose influence was exerted not so much by the actual exercise of its power as by its mere existence. Growing up under the shield of the silent presence of sea power, industrial civilization failed to recognize the importance of military force in general and tended for many decades to look upon it as an obsolete survival that would eventually disappear altogether.

Thus the whole structure of the new industrial culture was geared to peace, rather than to war, in a way that the older civilizations had never been. It was laid out according to criteria of maximum peacetime productivity and market competition. In contrast to pre-industrial civilizations, moreover, it was based upon greater and greater specialization, and thus tended to become more and more complex. Not only did it fuse the individual national economies into more and more interdependent structures; in expanding its activities around the world, it drew more and more countries into its network and in so doing became more and more dependent upon them.

The significance of this pattern did not become fully apparent as long as the military and civilian spheres remained essentially separate from each other. It required the outbreak of the First World War to shatter the illusions of peaceful progress in which the greater part of mankind had been living for the past hundred years. Thereafter, the sudden shift to an industrial basis of power once again brought the military and civilian spheres into intimate correlation and, in so doing, revealed the profound contradiction that had been developing between them.

It is true that with the new industrial and scientific base, military operations were freed of many of their most crippling limitations and achieved incomparably greater force, range, and versatility than at any time in the past. The sheer quantity of power that could be brought into play was staggeringly increased, not only in absolute terms but in the way it could be concentrated in time and space. Unlike power based on land and men, however, this new type of power rested on an infinitely more complex, specialized, and vulnerable foundation. Dependence on such an interrelated organization of resources can be tolerated in peacetime without too much disadvantage, despite the inherent weaknesses discussed in the preceding chapter. The breakdown of some isolated part of the elaborate machinery of living causes inconvenience but not catastrophe. But the situation in war is quite different. The more complex and vulnerable the base, the more precarious is the operation of the entire machine.

Given these inherent weaknesses, the twice-repeated reorientation of our whole industrial process from peaceful to wartime ends in the two World Wars was a much more remarkable achievement than is generally realized. Behind the masses of figures and picturesque details stood something much more imposing: the coordination and focusing upon common national objectives of the huge economic machines which had been in process of development for many decades, and which, in addition, had become increasingly involved with the intricate institutional networks of business corporations, labor unions, farmers' and professional organizations—institutions which were more accustomed to competition than to cooperation for common ends. Yet the effort to coordinate these sprawling elements was at best only partially successful. Organizations like the U.S. War Production Board and the Office of Price Administration developed into vast labyrinths that superimposed their own administrative intricacies upon those already existing in the economic fields they were created to coordinate. The sheer volume of paper work, the tabulating and analyzing of forms and questionnaires, created insurmountable difficulties. Industrial civilization had already become so vast and complicated that the administrative command posts could neither clearly survey the needs nor exercise effective control.

The critical importance and growing unwieldiness of the home base was matched by its greatly increased vulnerability to enemy attack. In the days when war was mainly a matter of men and ships, the home front was less important. A belligerent could still hope to win even if most of his own territory was overrun. But our new dependence on industrial means of warfare makes it indispensable not only to organize and coordinate the home base but to make sure that it will not suffer any vital disturbance. And this is all the more difficult because, as we have already pointed out, the peacetime development of industrial society is of a character that leaves it exceptionally vulnerable to such disruption even in normal times.

In the First World War this problem was left largely dormant by the immobilization of the front lines and the failure of air power effectively to disrupt the civilian war effort. The Allied naval blockade and the German submarine campaign were directed at the whole of the opponent's economic base, rather than concentrating against its critical spots. The Second World War brought the problem into much sharper focus. By this time the major belligerents were even more dependent on the continued operation of their industrial machines. On the Allied side, Great Britain survived only by reason of the Germans' failure fully to concentrate their attack upon any one of the various lines which, if resolutely pursued, might easily have proved fatal to the British capacity to wage war. The Russians, on their side, were saved in part by the width of their home front and by their foresight and resolution in evacuating their industrial installations from the Donets basin to the Urals and central Siberia; in part, also, by the restriction of the German air effort to the support of army operations and the failure to set in motion any strategic attack against the Russian industrial centers. The United States, thanks to its singularly fortunate geographic location, was not seriously endangered at any time, apart from the submarine attacks on shipping along the East Coast in the spring of 1942. Thus it was able to carry through its gigantic wartime mobilization practically undisturbed.

What these advantages meant can be seen from the contrasting experience of the Axis powers. In their initial campaigns, both Germany and Japan conquered broad territorial ramparts behind which they were able to mobilize their economies, almost as an afterthought, from 1942–43 onward. But the conquered territories afforded only temporary protection, and provided far less in the way of additional supplies than might have been possible. When the Allied naval and air attack got into its stride, the vulnerability of the German and Japanese war production centers soon became apparent.

Even so, it was only gradually that the Allied air strategy came to be directed at exploiting the inherent complexity and vulnerability of industrial society as it existed in the enemy countries. Germany had the advantage of an economy that had at least been partially mobilized. She also had a highly developed railway system and, despite increasingly effective Allied air attacks, managed to maintain sufficient rail transport to ensure the vital assembly of troops even for her final offensive in the Ardennes. But meanwhile her social structure and economy were going to pieces. The new type of submarines, built in sections, could not be assembled because the different pieces could not be brought together. Coordination between the various German armies broke down bit by bit.

The experience of Japan was even more significant. That country was doubly vulnerable to Allied attacks. It was a sea empire, and its naval communications were almost completely cut by a combination of naval and air action. The home islands, in turn, were completely dependent upon a few highly vulnerable coastal railways and upon coastal shipping. Even though air attack was not specifically concentrated upon these targets, by the end of the conflict Japan had been reduced to a state of widespread disorganization—cities burned out, communications cut, populations encamped in the countryside, industrial production virtually at a standstill, even the most elementary food supply endangered. This was the condition to which Japan had been reduced even before the dropping of the first atomic bombs on Hiroshima and Nagasaki inaugurated the new and still more awesome phase in the evolution of power that we know as the nuclear age.

THE MEANING OF NUCLEAR WEAPONS

Among the revolutionary developments of the years since 1945, none has made a deeper impression than the advent of nuclear weapons and their rapid emergence as the leading element in the war-making capacity of the major powers. This popular response has in most cases been deeply tinged with feelings of fear and revulsion. The unleashing of these blindly destructive forces is felt to threaten every advance, every gain that man has achieved in his prolonged upward struggle. Human progress, it is maintained, could go on to unlimited heights were it not for this satanic intrusion that seems so radically out of harmony with the otherwise hopeful course of our general evolution. Nuclear and thermonuclear weapons are felt to belong to a world entirely apart from man's other achievements. In their threat of utter and indiscriminate disaster, the crippling of future generations, and the breakdown of civilization itself, these weapons systems seem to elude any attempt at bringing them within the normal categories of human reason. From the standpoint of man's traditional orientation, they simply make no sense.

These extreme emotional reactions are as understandable as they are characteristic of our age's diffuse and fragmented mental outlook. It is quite true that in adding the force of the atom to his already formidable arsenal of power, man has taken a decisive and unprecedented step, one that cannot simply be accepted as another link in an unbroken chain of progress but requires a fundamental rethinking both of the questions of war and peace and of the whole problem of power and its uses. Where popular reaction tends to go astray is in its insistence on isolating the problem of nuclear weapons from the general evolution of industrial civilization. It is not only in the development of these particular weapons that man has surpassed his natural measure, and it is not simply by abolishing them, should that prove possible, that we shall achieve a saner and more ordered world. Our whole civilization has surpassed man's measure, and it is now our task to try to re-establish control over it in all its aspects, not simply in the most fearsome ones. It is within this broader framework that the particular problems raised by nuclear armaments must be viewed if there is to be any hope of resolving them.

What is really new in our crucial age is not merely the abrupt rise of our destructive powers to wholly unprecedented levels, but the rapid growth of the in-dwelling power inherent in *every* aspect of human activity, and the consequent conversion of all these activities into instruments of political and military significance. The increased power potential inseparable from even the most harmless and spontaneous activities becomes all the more significant because of the revolution wrought by nuclear weapons in the more limited field of military affairs proper. For the chief effect of nuclear weapons in the military field has been to limit in the most drastic fashion the possibility of their employment in war— or, indeed, of resorting to war at all as a means of safeguarding national interests or gaining national objectives.

From a purely military point of view, the most significant fact about the new weapons is that they have brought with them an increase in disruptive power so enormous that it threatens to overthrow the possibility of any concerted military strategy whatsoever. Strategy, in its broadest terms, is simply the coordination of all the elements of national life for purposes of attack or defense. Difficult enough at all times, the problems of such a total coordination were just beginning to be mastered as the result of the experience gained in the two World Wars, particularly the second. But the sudden appearance of weapons of such tremendous and concentrated power as the atomic and hydrogen bombs promptly wiped out this gain and created a strong possibility that the new-found coordination of resources, based primarily on new mechanical and electronic methods of transportation and communications, would be entirely nullified in any future war. More than this, it raised an acute threat that such a conflict would result in the disruption not only of the armed forces and the war effort *per se* but of the entire national organization.

It is in this threat of the disruption of a nation's entire life and activities under atomic attack that the true significance of the new weapons is to be found. The problem posed by nuclear bombardment is not simply one of millions or tens of millions of direct casualties. Beyond this lies the menace of a complete breakup of the intricate and vulnerable framework of industrial processes on which the life of any major country depends.

Industrial mobilization of the type that served in the two World Wars as a kind of inexhaustible cornucopia, pouring forth a stream of constantly modified and improved equipment, might be impossible to achieve in any future war. Nobody can foresee the kind of disruption pattern a nuclear bombardment would create, what vital parts of a national economy would be put out of action, and how the remaining resources could be reorganized. The same holds true of the key centers of any military effort, the naval and air bases and the great civilian ports. To some degree it holds true even of the operations of the field forces themselves. There is general agreement that the era of tremendous mass armies with their elaborate supply systems is past. The forces able to survive on a nuclear battlefield would have to be very much smaller, organized quite differently, and directed according to quite different principles, about which there are wide differences of opinion and no practical experience apart from tests conducted under peacetime conditions.

Like the famous symbol of the serpent biting its own tail, our industrial civilization has thus in a sense turned against itself. The tendency of industrial warfare ever since the First World War has been not merely toward the production of a greater volume of munitions but toward a greater, more concentrated striking power. With the atomic bomb and the technically unlimited series of weapons that it inaugurated, modern warfare has reached the point at which it threatens its own complex and vulnerable bases with fatal disruption. Industrial power threatens to destroy its own roots.

We need not conclude that the self-defeating nature of the new weapons will necessarily prevent their ever being used. The circumstances under which they could still be brought into play are too numerous and too easily imagined for us to indulge in any easy illusions on this score. What we can say, however, is that the very nature of the new weapons, in conjunction with their availability to members of both of the leading power groups in the contemporary world, represents a powerful deterrent to their use by either side. With such weapons in the background, there is a strong tendency to try to prevent even "conventional" military operations from reaching a degree of intensity that could seriously threaten their "escalation" into nuclear war.

This, however, is merely another way of saying that the most significant effect of the new weapons has been a radical change in the whole relationship between the military, political, and other forms of power. Up to the dawn of the nuclear age, the relations between different peoples had always been determined ultimately by the decisive nature of military power as the final arbitrament from which there was no appeal. War was the *ultima ratio regis,* the ultimate argument of a ruler. In the new conditions created by the development of nuclear weapons, this simply no longer holds. The conditions under which a modern government can seriously contemplate a resort to war against a nuclear-armed opponent are limited, for all practical purposes, to the eventuality of a direct attack on some absolutely vital interest.

Nonmilitary forms of rivalry, such as economic competition or political subversion, no longer seem to afford clear justification for such a frightful risk. Even direct military aggression against objectives of secondary importance may be found too inconsequential to warrant a full-scale nuclear response, as has been evidenced more than once by the postwar history of the Far East.

What this means is that political rivalry has been released from the ultimate control by military power that prevailed in all earlier epochs. Since militarily the available deterrents lead to a stalemate, the field is thrown wide open to the use of the nonmilitary forces of political, economic, and psychological rivalry. To put it another way, the mutual possession of nuclear weapons has brought with it a radical change in the development of power relations between states. Not armed forces alone, but every other element in the civilizations of the rival powers now becomes an essential factor in the struggle. The leading powers confront each other not only with troops, bombs, and missiles, but with such potent nonmilitary weapons as radio transmitters, moon rockets, trade and aid programs, drama and ballet groups, hockey and chess teams, youth and peace congresses.

The implications of this transformation become more readily apparent if one looks at the peculiar political configuration that has helped to give these novel instruments of warfare their present decisive importance.

The Limits of Peaceful Coexistence

The emergence of the Soviet Union as one of the undisputed leaders among the world powers had implications no less far-reaching than those of the invention of nuclear weapons and the establishment, at almost the same time, of the United Nations as an international political organization explicitly designed to obviate the use or threat of force in international affairs and "save succeeding generations from the scourge of war." As the product of a Communist revolution and the official heir to the ideological tradition inaugurated by Karl Marx, the Soviet Government brought to world affairs a point of view that differed radically from that of contemporary non-Communist governments. For the latter, war and peace had traditionally represented two distinct and clearly differentiated states, peace being accepted more or less as the normal condition of international affairs while war remained an exceptional state that was entered into only under extraordinary and pressing circumstances.

Soviet thinking reversed these concepts—or, rather, it substituted for the idea of alternating states of war and peace the notion of a continuing, unappeasable conflict in which the forces of Communism were constantly pitted against those of the capitalist world in a merciless war to the death. With the victory of the Bolshevik party in Russia in 1917, the Marxian doctrine of class struggle had simply been extended from the national to the international level. Peace in any real sense between the upholders of the capitalist order and its Communist challengers was held to be out of the question. "We are living not merely in a state but in a system of states," Lenin had written in 1919, "and the existence of the Soviet Republic side by side with imperialist states for a long time is unthinkable. One or the other must triumph in the end. And before that end supervenes, a series of frightful collisions between the Soviet Republic and the bourgeois states will be inevitable."

This commitment to an unremitting struggle for the final world-wide victory of Communism made it quite impossible for Communist governments to accept in good faith the obligations of United Nations membership. For the Soviet Union and its associates, the new organization was not so much "a center for harmonizing the actions of nations" as a medium for the furtherance of specifically Communist, or Soviet, interests. It goes without saying that the other members of the United Nations have also done their best to use its potentialities to protect and advance their own interests. With the exception of the Communist members, however, this pursuit of specialized national interests has generally been carried on within the limits of a broad respect for the principles of the Charter and the authority of U.N. bodies. Had the U.S.S.R. and its associated governments brought to their participation in the United Nations even the limited spirit of accommodation displayed by most of their non-Communist fellow members, the organization would have had at least a reasonable chance of accomplishing the major purposes for which it was established.

Under the actual circumstances prevailing since 1945, the United Nations has been able to deal effectively with only a limited range of international conflicts, principally those outbreaks of fighting among smaller powers that the Soviet Union itself had no more interest in perpetuating than did its Western opponents. To discourage armed conflict among the great powers themselves, the world has been forced to rely primarily on more traditional means. We have been thrown back on something very like the much maligned balance-of-power system that reached its apogee toward the end of the pre-industrial age.

The present situation, however, differs from that of the classical period of the balance of power in two vital respects. Instead of a large number of competing power centers that could align and realign themselves in various patterns in response to changing circumstances, through most of the postwar period there have been but two major powers, the U.S.S.R. and the U.S., each flanked by a number of allies and associates of widely varying military strength and significance. Second, and even more important, whereas in the classical period of the balance of power it was the prerogative of any state that felt its interests threatened to resort to war at any moment it judged favorable, in the age of nuclear weapons this method of protecting national interests is no longer generally available.

The historical balance of power based on physical and human resources has thus been superseded by a "balance of terror" in which the price of resorting to arms has become altogether too high to be contemplated under normal circumstances. No longer able to count on an opportunity to mobilize their resources after a conflict starts, the opposing forces must expect to stake every-thing upon their already existing means of attack. Standing poised against each other, each of the potential combatants is capable of pounding his enemy to rubble and throwing his political, admin-istrative, economic, and social systems into chaos—but each seems almost inevitably doomed to suffer the same fate in the process.

The nations of the world were slow to grasp the implications of this momentous change in their power relations. Not until some ten years after the close of the Second World War did the leaders of the major powers begin to acknowledge that the advent of nuclear weapons had completely outmoded the traditional method of settling international disputes and necessitated the de-velopment of new methods of adjusting international differences. In the case of the Soviet Union, this avowal went hand in hand with the enunciation by Nikita S. Khrushchev of a policy of "peaceful coexistence" explicitly aimed at bringing about the es-tablishment of a Communist world without incurring the risks of large-scale military conflict.

From the standpoint of Communist traditions, this change of methods was less revolutionary than it seemed. Communism, de-spite its frankly militant character, its emphasis on inevitable con-flict, and its versatile use of military forces as an instrument of policy, had always remained essentially a political rather than a military movement. Marx himself had conceived of Communism in terms of an all-embracing coordination of the most different activities and points of view—philosophical, economic, social, po-litical, and psychological—all of which could be brought to bear upon the key issue of the expansion of power and the danger of the self-alienation of man. This breadth of approach, which sought to place the Communist revolution within the context of the en-tire development of mankind, gave and still gives to Communists a world-historical perspective that has been largely lacking to other political movements. This combination of a world perspec-tive and an all-inclusive political approach has endowed Com-munism with the crucial trait in which it has so greatly surpassed all other regimes, either democratic or totalitarian: namely, the systematic mobilization and coordination of all spheres of human thought and activity as means to a single political objective.

It is this systematic organization of all the different fields of human endeavor that represents the unique force of the Communist revolutionary strategy. Within that strategy the armed forces have a highly respected role. But their function is simply to provide the ultimate backing for this wider, concerted revolutionary effort that involves the systematic employment of a wide variety of nonmilitary techniques—political, diplomatic, economic, and psychological. In other words, it involves a concentrated and systematic exploitation of the various forms of nonmilitary power built up by the industrial revolution and disciplined and coordinated by the all-embracing Marxist view of human affairs.

Not the least of the advantages of such a strategy of "peaceful coexistence" or "peaceful competition" was the comparative unpreparedness of the Western world to recognize and meet the challenge. Psychologically, the Western peoples were far better prepared for outright military conflict than they were for this new type of war without arms. Nurtured for centuries on the idea of a strict separation between the nonpolitical, private sphere and the political, public sphere, between "war" on one side and "peace" on the other, they found it most difficult to grasp the fact that with the universal expansion of power in our age, every aspect of activity has come to play a political role and assume political overtones.

At least initially, therefore, the tendency in the West was to assume that if the extreme danger of a thermonuclear conflict could be avoided, the deployment of these nonmilitary forces constituted no real threat to Western interests. Western authorities even professed to welcome any tendency to shift the East-West conflict into areas in which they felt so well able to hold their own. But though the superiority in numbers, in economic power, and particularly in the diversity of spiritual forces still lies with the West, this superiority has not been organized as it has been in the military sphere. While in agreement with respect to the repulsing of an armed attack, the Western governments art not in accord to the same extent on their political interests and economic policies. Their common front thus offers many openings for skillful pressures aimed at confusing and dividing them. At the same time, their potential strength in the non-military field has remained almost entirely unmobilized.

Whatever Khrushchev's personal convictions and intentions, moreover, in a world as deeply divided as ours it is difficult to imagine a competition that could remain permanently restricted to the psychological and economic levels. Competition even in these fields inevitably involves a buildup of power, with all the dangers that this implies. Furthermore, the psychological-economic struggle that the Soviet leaders have so persistently advocated is not simply a sporting test. As Khrushchev himself has never failed to emphasize, it is a struggle of the two systems for political survival. We have yet to learn whether a great power whose political survival is really at stake will be content to leave the outcome to nonmilitary processes as long as stronger methods are still available.

There remains the much-discussed possibility that the Soviet Union and the other Communist powers will tacitly renounce their oft-proclaimed goal of world revolution and thus open the way to a real and permanent "coexistence" with the peoples of the free world. Despite the wholly negative character of the Marxist doctrine on this point, we need not conclude that the present-day Marxist regimes are inevitably committed to struggle on until Communism has been spread to the four corners of the globe. On the military side, the development of the nuclear stalemate has already foreclosed the possibility of a successful world revolution along old-style Marxist lines. Communism, while freed of the apprehension of being crushed that haunted its leaders for a generation or more, has also lost any prospect of achieving its own goal of world revolution by military means.

The changes in the political sphere have been equally far-reaching. The original Marxist doctrine, already subjected to a series of extensive reinterpretations in the hands of Lenin and others, has had to be increasingly stretched out and "relativized" in order to fit it to the widely varying circumstances prevailing in a large number of Communist-ruled countries. Concurrently, the original revolutionary leadership in the U.S.S.R. and other Communist states has been gradually supplanted by a new, professionally trained elite that seems less concerned with promoting world revolution than with the execution of concrete administrative and managerial tasks and, above all, the consolidation of its own privileged position.

But while these developments may have led to some dilution of Communism's original revolutionary drive, it would be foolish to overlook the dominant position maintained by the Communist parties, with their doctrinaire Marxist commitment, in all branches of society. Any "mellowing" of Communism that the coming years may hold in store is therefore unlikely to proceed as rapidly as most of us would like to believe. Above all, it cannot in the nature of things be an openly avowed process. The ultimate goal of world revolution is so fundamental to Communism that it cannot be publicly repudiated even after its leaders have come to realize that it is no longer practically possible.

The situation is further complicated by the fact that the two key Communist states of the present day, the U.S.S.R. and China, are in radically different stages of development and have correspondingly differing aims. In the former country, Communism has passed its initial virulent stage; it is now second-generation Communism. In its rapidly increasing material development, the U.S.S.R. has great sources of strength but no compelling need for an aggressive expansionist policy. In Communist China, on the other hand, Communism is new, still in its first generation, and still directed by the men who actually established it. Potentially an industrial giant, China at the present time is not as well off economically as the United States, the Soviet Union, or in some respects even India. Its spectacular advances during its first decade under Communism were due primarily to the energy of its leaders in organizing and coordinating mass manpower to a much greater degree than was achieved by collectivization in the Soviet Union. The very intensity of this process has created in the Chinese system a dynamism that is quite exceptional even for our age. It has also made for a far more intransigent ideological outlook than in the Soviet Union, as well as a far more dynamic form of expansionism in foreign policy.

These differences are accentuated by the differences in the international position and experience of the two regimes. For more than a generation the Soviet Union has been an influential member of the community of nations. The Chinese Communist struggle for survival was much more prolonged and desperate, and has not yet been crowned by similar international acknowledgment. Even after gaining control over the whole of the China mainland in 1949, the new regime found itself almost completely isolated internationally. Primarily as the result of their intervention against the United Nations forces in Korea, the Chinese Communists have so far been shut out from the community of nations, from its cooperative activities as well as the opportunity to exchange opinions which membership affords. The antagonism of the Chinese Communist Government toward the countries of the West in general and the United States in particular is one of the most basic facts of the present world situation. It is probably the most serious of all the obstacles to any genuine relaxation of tensions, and hence the most serious of all the existing threats to world peace.

Confronted by the spectacle of a world divided into hostile camps and poised on the brink of suicidal conflict, many have found comfort in reflecting that the bloody and seemingly no less irreconcilable conflicts between Christians and Muslims, Catholics and Protestants did after all give way eventually to a state of mutual tolerance. But this analogy tends to overlook two vital facts. At the level of power then prevailing, Christians and Muslims, Catholics and Protestants could perhaps afford to indulge in these fantastic bloodlettings until sheer exhaustion brought them to reason. Our incomparably higher level of power no longer permits us to do so.

However fanatically these religious factions might quarrel with one another, moreover, they differed from our present-day antagonists in that they still believed in observing some measure of good faith toward friends and adversaries alike. Because in their different ways they all acknowledged some underlying truths, the need for some degree of veracity in human relations, there was a basis on which a state of mutual tolerance and coexistence could be reconstituted.

The most destructive work of Communism lies precisely in the thoroughness with which it has sought to demolish any belief in the possibility of faith or truth between the representatives of antagonistic social systems, not to mention the relations between rulers and ruled within the Communist states themselves. At least a minimum of good faith, affording some degree of assurance against manipulation, perversion, and deception, must be recovered if mankind is to go on, even though it can no longer be the naïve faith of man in man that tended to prevail in all traditional societies. It would be no service to the cause of East-West understanding to delude ourselves about the difficulty of what may well be the most critical of all the problems of contemporary international affairs.

THE CONTROL OF WAR POTENTIAL

The uncertain attitude of Communist China would be enough in itself to demonstrate the impossibility of treating the existing military stalemate as a convenient cushion on which to relax. At most it offers a period of relative stability, a breathing spell in which to tackle the complex political and military problems involved in establishing a more stable kind of coexistence. Thus it is not surprising that political and military discussion in recent years has tended to focus primarily on the objective of "stabilizing" the existing state of mutual deterrence in the hope that some check can be imposed on the international arms race and that the general political situation in the world can be prevented from deteriorating further. While it is difficult to quarrel with such an objective, it should be realized that a state of mutual deterrence, even if capable of being stabilized, would present quite serious problems and would be very far indeed from total reliability under all circumstances.

It is frequently forgotten that the new balance of military power is far more psychological than physical or material in character. Attack by one side or the other is deterred not so much by the physical strength of the defense as by the psychological inhibition exercised by the threat of retaliation. This inhibition, however, can operate only if it is assumed that under extreme conditions the opponent would actually be willing to face the hazards of nuclear warfare, even though it would most probably mean his own extinction. The state of relative stability and security in which we exist today depends not merely upon the fact that each side has the necessary force to annihilate the other, but equally upon the mutual conviction that there are situations in which the other side might actually make use of these weapons regardless of consequences.

Furthermore, the state of mutual deterrence is the reverse of a static condition. The rough equilibrium that now exists between the major power groups is continually being subjected to many kinds of pressures which could, singly or collectively, have the effect of upsetting it altogether. The first of these pressures is the stress of the arms race itself—the unrestrained competition in the development of more and more powerful missiles, aircraft, submarines, antimissile systems, and other weapons, combined with the entry of new countries into the competition. Behind these phenomena is the constant flow of scientific and technological discoveries and innovations, many of which have a military significance that in some instances may be potentially decisive.

Equally significant, though much less frequently noticed, is the rapidly increasing power of the various nonmilitary forces of which so much has been said in this book. The present politico-military struggle involves not only the exercise of power in the traditional sense, but also a wide variety of other forces—industrial, commercial, cultural, psychological—that were developed for quite different purposes but have been increasingly brought within the scope of a universal power rivalry. These highly varied components of the power equation, all of them in process of rapid and simultaneous development, could lead by their joint impact to a fatal weakening of the present state of mutual deterrence.

The most serious complaint that can be raised with respect to the disarmament negotiations carried on during the past fifteen years or more is their neglect of precisely these factors. In concentrating almost exclusively on what may be called the *tactical* and *technical* problems of arms control, they have failed to penetrate beyond them to the key *strategic* problems resulting from the dynamic march of events. Almost ignored up to now has been the problem created by the various elements of political, economic, psychological, and cultural rivalry, as well as the explosive population pressures developing at certain points of the globe.

Only in very recent years have there been signs of a dawning realization of the potential significance of these forces, together with some rather piecemeal and haphazard attempts at establishing "ground rules" to regulate international competition in at least some nonmilitary areas. Joint efforts have been initiated in such fields as the peaceful uses of nuclear energy, the exploration of the Antarctic, and the investigation of outer space. Such initiatives reflect a definite effort to lessen the intensity of competition by getting the rival groups around a table to discuss the issues and seek cooperative rather than competitive procedures. There are undoubtedly dangers in this method of trying to work out differences and conflicts of interest. Joint efforts would not be equally successful in all fields. But the general idea is at least worth encouraging as one possible approach to the vital problem of finding common ground among the competing world powers.

A second strategic point in regulating the impact of our greatly expanded power in the international field is the need for some reserve powers that would ultimately be removed from the direct control of the major international contestants. No system of direct controls over armaments or other forms of power can ever be expected to work perfectly. In view of the many loopholes in different spheres of activity, we simply cannot rely upon any set of direct controls that might be devised. There has to be something in reserve to back up any body of tactical and technical controls that may be agreed upon. It is very questionable, however, whether the magnitude of the problems arising in this connection has been adequately recognized. In order to restrain effectively any evasion of agreed control measures or any resort to biological or chemical warfare or as yet unknown forms of scientific warfare, the reserve powers would have to be organized in such a way that they could be brought into action promptly and upon a global scale. In the present state of our development, this inevitably means that long-range thermonuclear weapons would have to be held in reserve for this purpose. Initially, moreover, they would undoubtedly have to be held by the nuclear powers themselves, since there is no other authority to which they could conceivably be entrusted either politically or practically.

It is at this point that the popular desire for disarmament clashes most sharply with the realistic requirements of any arms-control system. People everywhere have felt that the most vital and immediate task is to ban and abolish nuclear arms as the very first step toward a more livable world. In reality, if any reliable system of arms control is to be established, the removal of nuclear and thermonuclear weapons from the world scene would have to be not the first step but the last. This does not mean that nothing can be done in the meantime to lessen the fear of a thermonuclear conflict. The mere fact of an international agreement on a system of arms control would serve to reduce mutual apprehensions, together with the accompanying danger that these weapons might be used inadvertently through the misreading of an opponent's intentions. Thus a way would also be opened toward working out means of eventually placing the indispensable reserve forces under international authority when and if a reliable authority can be constituted.

A third fundamental point in any program for arms control or disarmament is the fact that disarmament cannot be accomplished by a single act or a predetermined series of phases but must be in the nature of a continuous process. All proposals so far advanced tend to treat disarmament essentially as a one-, two-, or three-phased operation in which the existing armed forces are eliminated or cut down to police levels under a single comprehensive program. This type of proposal is, however, directed only toward the more immediate forms of military power, involving clearly limited and defined forces that could conceivably be abolished by a single action or set of actions. This, as we have repeatedly pointed out, is only part of our problem. We cannot abolish the power that is virtually coextensive with the whole of our civilization, and that continues to develop and expand in quite unforeseeable ways. Efforts to control it must therefore be perpetual, and each new generation will have to deal with the new problems that will inevitably arise.

In sum, the purpose of any system of disarmament must be to establish a basis for the continuous control of power; it cannot eliminate its presence in our kind of society. Once a plan for arms control has been agreed upon and set up, it would not remain an isolated and firmly established fact. In the place of our present arms race based upon the precarious safeguard of mutual deterrence, it would simply establish a controlled and stabilized framework of armed power that would provide the starting point for an indefinite series of further modifications as new sources of power are developed.

Under such a system we could either gradually transfer the present standing forces to other public functions or reduce and perhaps eventually eliminate them. We could deal in similar fashion with the difficult problem of redirecting our industrial power from arms production to other forms of productive activity. But let us be clear that in so doing we would not be eliminating the problem of power as such. Disarmament is a beginning, not an end. Instead of pursuing the *fata morgana* of a radical elimination of power once and for all, let us direct our efforts to the establishment of a flexible system of *controlling* power, however much it may continue to increase or expand in the future and whatever unforeseen shapes it may yet assume.

6

Toward the Mastery
of Power

SINCE THE TIME of the Renaissance and the religious
schism, Western civilization has been continually
moving forward. The period since 1500 has brought
rapid and continuous progress in all the forms of political, economic, and social organization, in education and the development of the mind, in medical care and understanding, in science
and technology. In contrast to earlier civilizations, confined by
their traditions to certain predetermined lines of development,
the uninhibited freedom that distinguishes the Western mind has
resulted in a measureless fanning out and interaction of all
branches of thought and activity. This interaction among the
many separate fields of Western development has itself been a
powerful spur to further advances. In some cases, notably in the
realm of science, there has been an increasing cross-fertilization
between different lines of progress. In others, as in the growing
development of large metropolitan areas, there has been an actual
convergence or intertwining of the various factors contributing
to growth.

Thus our age is characterized by a constantly expanding stream of new thoughts, cultural energies, material resources. This flood of experiences, discoveries, and potentialities has become so overwhelming in its breadth and diversity that it is growing more and more difficult even to "take in," let alone appreciate its true significance for our lives and those of future generations.

THE NEW DIMENSIONS OF POWER

The schizophrenic character of our age is nowhere more clearly reflected than in the diametrically opposite interpretations to which these phenomena are subjected. On one side, it is uncritically hailed as a time of dizzying progress; on the other, it is just as uncritically bemoaned as an era of decadence, decline, and cultural "massification." This divided outlook, moreover, is no mere transitional phenomenon, to be explained by saying that we have simply been overwhelmed by the onrush of industrial civilization and need time to find our bearings and establish ourselves on a new level of power. On the contrary, it is in keeping with the basic character of our age, which is itself divided in its innermost nature.

As we contemplate the vast possibilities that have been placed in our hands by our growing mastery over nature, it is no wonder that our first instinctive feeling is a sense of freedom such as men have never before experienced. For the first time, it seems, man is no longer condemned to live essentially on a subsistence level. He seems to hold within his grasp the power to do away with all the burdens, wants, and fears that have hitherto weighed upon him. Comparing his present situation with the severely limited power he wielded in earlier times, he may well be tempted by the illusion that he now possesses absolute power and has achieved a genuinely independent position in relation to nature.

Yet the feeling of release that is so prevalent in our age would be unbalanced and dangerous if we failed to realize that this new freedom which man has achieved cannot by its very nature be unlimited. The power of man is not, and can never become, absolute. He remains a limited being. As the traditional limitations imposed by nature are overcome, new cultural limitations arise in their stead. Power does not free us from limiting counterforces, and never will; at most it may give us a somewhat greater latitude in choosing the limitations we will accept.

But if it is a mistake to view our age as a time of unqualified advance, it is no less erroneous to regard it as a period of decadence—particularly if we follow the fashionable example of a Spengler or a Toynbee and try to equate it with one or more limited periods in the development of the High Civilizations, such as the period of Hellenism and the Roman Empire. The crisis of our age is essentially a crisis of progress, not of decadence. The fact that it may lead to catastrophe is not in itself a proof of decadence, but only of its critical character.

This critical character of our age results directly from the inward break in the relationship between man and nature that accompanied our emergence from the agricultural into the industrial stage of human development. The radical change in man's relationship to the world around him is, in fact, the decisive characteristic of the industrial age. Whereas the agricultural period was essentially a time of consolidation of man within the world, in the industrial stage this consolidating tendency has been decisively interrupted. For the first time, man's independence vis-à-vis nature has risen to the level of consciousness. His assertion of independence has in sober fact reached a point at which a simple reintegration is no longer conceivable.

Instead of an ever-increasing consolidation within nature, mankind's advance from the agricultural to the industrial stage has led to the disclosure of a fundamental and ever-increasing *tension* between man and nature—a tension that can never be definitively mastered but must continue to increase with the continuing increase in man's own power. Our entrance into the industrial stage, in other words, has led not to a consummation of the fundamental tendency of the agricultural stage but rather to its exact opposite.

This constantly increasing tension is the direct result of the tremendous surge of power of every kind that is generated by the diverse activities of our industrial civilization. The growth of power in our era has reached a point at which mere quantity may be said to have turned into quality, effecting a qualitative transformation in the whole character of our civilization. This transformation, which brings with it problems with respect to the recognition, control, and integration of power of a wholly different magnitude from those that confronted Hegel and Marx, is still proceeding irresistibly. In another fifty years at most it will have involved not merely the present industrialized powers but the entire world.

However often we may succeed in temporarily mastering the varied tensions in which the growth of our power entangles us, all our solutions are bound to remain conditional and limited in character. The increase in power in future years will undoubtedly be subject to limitation at various points—as in the limitation of our living space—but as a whole it will nevertheless continue. We shall continue to desire, and to create, new things; and, in so doing, to create new power. Thus we shall constantly be faced anew with the problem of how these new forms of power can be subjected to our control. The tension between the creation of power by man and the question of his control over this power stands revealed in the industrial age as the basic problem of all human development.

This state of affairs differs from all past experience in another fundamental way. The great upheavals in man's previous development have invariably been brought about by man himself, through active exertions which, at the same time, brought into being the spiritual forces required for the intellectual control of the new world he was creating. The present upheaval, in contrast, is one that is essentially not so much willed as passively experienced. In surrendering to the inertia of the forces we have unleashed, we have failed to create the means of maintaining our mastery over them.

Faced with this widening gap between reality and our capacity for understanding it, our tendency has been simply to resign, to abandon the attempt at dominating our situation. With the introduction of more and more masses of men into the new industrial processes, we have habituated ourselves to an unthinking acceptance of their continued operation. The tremendous increase in destructive force, especially in atomic weapons, has led to an inward capitulation before the whole problem of the control of power. This is the real root of present-day conformity and political apathy. As a result, the really astounding developments of our time are received by the broad masses with every evidence of indifference and boredom. Since men's spiritual forces are no longer stimulated in any important degree, we are met by a deceptive appearance of spiritual exhaustion and decadence.

Thus the transition from the agricultural to the industrial stage is characterized by a twofold process working in opposite directions. On one side, the radical posing of the problem of man's power has highlighted the necessity of not abandoning human processes to their own automatism but of mastering and governing them through a series of responsible decisions. On the other side, as a result of the varied influences of the industrial stage, both the understanding and the capacity for this guidance have greatly declined. Instead of seeking the responsible *control* of power, men have almost invariably preferred to follow the false trail that supposedly leads to its radical elimination.

EVASION AND REALITY

It is the peoples of the West who are primarily responsible for these evasions. For the evolution of mankind to its present level of power has been essentially the work of the West, not only in its later stages but from its earliest beginnings with the Prophets of Israel and the Greeks. The history of the West has been an uninterrupted struggle with the problem of power and of man's mastery over this power—which is another name for freedom. It is not just a history of the physical, naturalistic striving for power that has existed everywhere and at all times. Rather it is the history of a struggle over the principles of power, the nature of power, the control of power; a struggle over power not only among personalities but among objective forces—between church and state, among the states, and among groups within the state, between the executive, the legislative, and the judicial powers. It has been a struggle over a clear definition of the spheres of public and private interest and the relationship between them.

This great tradition of power has shaped the West in its political forms and in its political ideas; and from the West it has made its mark upon the rest of the world. Yet as we contemplate this towering political tradition, we are forced to ask ourselves how far it really remains alive and how far it has degenerated into a mere passive inheritance, a purely formal legacy as distinct from a conscious and living heritage. To what extent are we, who still live in the political forms of this tradition and use its language, aware of how these forms and this language arose and how they have changed? How far are we ourselves still involved in this struggle? If it is true that the West has struggled with the problem of power more than all other civilizations, does this problem of power still remain as living and central for the West as it has been in the course of its long development?

The question is complex. Yet it is difficult to escape the impression that the problem of power in this larger sense is no longer automatically recognized as a significant issue in the Western world. Concern with power has been heavily diluted by the growth of democracy, which is conventionally regarded less as a method of regulating power relationships within the state than as a means of eliminating power altogether from the field of public affairs. The prevailing tendency is to regard democracy as a kind of glorified "private sphere" which, by definition, is looked upon as free from the disturbing element of power.

A similar conception has been carried over into the field of international relations. The international order embodied in the

League of Nations and, more fully, in the United Nations is regarded less as a mechanism for the adjustment of power tensions
than as a means for the adjustment of problems that are conceived
essentially in a juridical manner. With the restriction of the role
of the Security Council, the element of power that was still present
in the original concept of the United Nations is increasingly
passed over. Every effort is made to act as though it played no part
in the various controversies brought before the organization.
Through its claim to have effected an identification between
power and law, the United Nations has tended to strengthen the
impression that the element of power as such is being successfully
eliminated from the field of interstate relations.

To an increasing extent the thinking of the West has turned
aside from these traditional conceptions to abandon itself to the
overpowering wave of industrial civilization. And, as this wave
becomes more and more overwhelming, the problem of power that
is inherent in it continues to be completely overlooked. Public
questions, the world itself is looked upon as something to be reduced to an aggregation of private problems. Public forms—
democracy within the state, legal order between the states—are
considered useful only in order to ensure the development of production and consumption by fundamentally excluding power. Desiring nothing so much as to get away from power altogether, the
Western peoples appear determined to misconceive its nature and
to look on it as something essentially separate, or at least sepa-
rable, from life.

The attitudes prevailing in the non-Western world are scarcely
more realistic. Except for its insistence on a prior settlement of
the class struggle, the Communist view is essentially akin to that
of the West. In the Communist nations, as in the West, the ultimate ideal is a world in which there are no more public problems
but only an "administration of things." As for the peoples of the
resurgent countries, their negative view of the whole concept of
power results directly from their habit of equating power with
colonialism.

All of these attitudes rest on a common belief, explicit or implicit, in the possibility of eliminating power from human affairs. All of them are equally oblivious of the fact that the problem of power is really the fundamental problem of our time and will remain the basic problem of all future history, no matter what the outcome of the present international struggle. Yet despite this almost universal self-deception, one thing is certain: the problem of power will not come to rest, but will force itself more and more urgently upon us. It will be more urgent in 1970 than in 1960, and more urgent still in 1980. By the year 2000 it will be the dominating public problem.

THE LEVELS OF RESPONSIBILITY

It need scarcely be repeated, then, that the basic requirement of the industrial age is a radical readjustment in man's relationship to power, one that would endow him with a will and a capability for mastering it that would correspond to the overwhelming power he has learned to unleash. We cannot abolish power; we can only try to control it.

Furthermore, we cannot control it absolutely. Power has roots that not only are independent of all reason, but are fundamentally not subject to its influence. All civilizations have endeavored in one way or another to arrive at a reconciliation between reason and power, between right and might. But the reconciliation of these two antithetical elements has always been a temporary and conditional one, limited to concrete cases, rather than a definitive reconciliation "in principle." The tendency of our age to think in terms of absolute solutions, though encountered in all the different camps that are concerned with power, is basically self-defeating. A recognition of the fundamentally unreasonable character of power, and of the fact that in consequence its control can never be made absolute and perfect, is the basis of all control.

It need scarcely be added that the problem of power and its control is not ordinarily raised in such comprehensive terms. In our day, attention has focused almost exclusively on the single issue of atomic weapons. This emphasis has been entirely justified in the sense that the problem of atomic weapons really is of basic significance for the survival and further development of mankind. But it has been unjustified and misleading insofar as it has encouraged the belief that this special problem, lying within the specialized field of military power, is coextensive with the general problem of power and its control—and that with its solution the whole problem of power would be solved once for all. We have already seen that in reality this would not be true even in the specialized field of military power. It would not in any way affect the complex of problems involved in the general increase of power, which is just as comprehensive as the development of human civilization itself and just as incapable of being circumscribed and regulated in advance.

The fact is that the problem of the increase of power is both universal and continuing, and that its solution must be equally universal and continuing. We must attack the problem not at haphazard but systematically.

The question therefore arises as to just who can and should tackle this problem that so greatly transcends all previous experience. Our first thought, naturally, is of governments. Throughout man's development, it is essentially the governments that have been charged with the continuing, responsible, and public regulation and adjustment of the power elements which have assembled and begun to collide with each other within any single group of people. To the extent that the problem of the public regulation of power is encountered within a national framework, this will continue to be the case in future, except that the scope of the regulatory activity of governments will necessarily have to increase along with the increase in power itself.

This, however, is by no means true of all of the power problems that have hitherto been resolved essentially by and between governments. A very essential result of the extension of human power is the emergence of certain problems which, since they affect all peoples, can be resolved only by general agreement. Whereas in earlier times the natural center for the control of power was the political community, the state, the overwhelming increase and generalization of power in the industrial stage has begun to point the way to a new and more complex division of responsibility. Its much broader character reflects the distinction between three elements: the great power-control problems which affect mankind as a whole, and which can only be solved with any prospect of success by mankind as a whole; the national problems of power control, which must continue to fall to the state; and the innumerable private and social power problems whose solution is a matter for individuals and social groups.

Those problems that concern mankind as a whole are something essentially new and peculiar to our era. Hitherto, the earth's resources were not so systematically claimed, relations between the individual states were not so closely interwoven, the power of these states was not so overwhelming as to prevent the resultant power tensions from being dealt with in the same manner as other interstate controversies.

Today, however, the situation is radically different. The living space of our planet is being continually filled by the growth of population, which is coming to represent a political problem of increasing significance because of the pressure of the densely populated areas on the less populous ones. The same is true of raw materials, which with today's heavy demands are beginning to be exhausted at an alarming rate. If the danger of an immediate shortage has been staved off by the revolutionary discoveries of nuclear chemistry and the shift from richer to less and less rich yields, the reorientation of production and consumption nevertheless requires a planned management which, from a point of view extending over several generations, can be carried out only on a basis determined by all nations in common.

The same tendency is apparent with respect to that element which has hitherto been distinguished precisely by its characteristic of freedom and accessibility to all—namely, the sea. To the extent that the exploration and economic exploitation of the sea increase, a new complex of problems demanding international regulation will develop here too. Of the same order are the problems of outer space, whose exploration similarly represents a common concern of mankind.

Another area where some measure of international regulation is clearly required is that of the relations among nations. The more closely these relations are knit, the more necessary will be the establishment of certain minimum rights that the nations must reciprocally concede to each other and to their nationals. These problems are made all the more urgent by the revolution in interstate relations and in the coexistence of the different states that has developed from the growth and extension of our powers of destruction. Beyond this, we shall also have to deal with the changes in national attitudes that are occurring as the result of the closer contact among the states and their populations.

Sober, practical consideration leaves no doubt that all of these matters concern not only the individual states or groups of states but the collective humanity that is now in process of formation. It is equally apparent that in view of the conflicts and dangers which a failure to regulate them will certainly conjure up sooner or later, a timely common regulation would be in the general interest even if all concerned must in the process make certain sacrifices involving some limitation of their complete freedom of action.

Our age, however, is not favorable to the adoption of such sober, objective attitudes toward its necessary demands. Our special difficulty lies in the fact that in addition to having to struggle with novel concrete problems of unprecedented magnitude, we find ourselves enmeshed in a network of emotional inhibitions and conflicts which make every concrete solution extremely difficult if not impossible. In part these inhibitions reflect the deep-rooted attitudes of the peoples toward each other, their national traditions and interests, the traditional emphasis on the independence of one's own state and the resultant mistrust of every arrangement that involves a limitation of this independence. Such influences from the past are intensified by the passionate nature of the contemporary conflicts between the free states and the Communist one-party states, and between the Western states and the newly resurgent peoples.

If these problems are to be confronted with any prospect of success, we shall clearly have to overcome the tendency to assume that it is impossible to negotiate with people with whom one disagrees until the latter abandon their most cherished convictions. Communism is not likely to change its underlying assumptions; and even if it should do so, its leaders would still have to reassert them in public. Yet our world cannot possibly stand still until this long-drawn-out process has reached its end. We shall not only have to negotiate with Communism, but to deal with it, even while recognizing that it still seeks the destruction of our form of society. The more ways we can find of dealing with it, the better our prospects of inducing it to move away from those belligerent traits that presently stand out as insuperable obstacles to any re-establishment of trust and genuine cooperation.

As we confront these long-range prospects, we are entitled to draw encouragement from the underlying tendencies that begin to reveal themselves as mankind increasingly transcends its traditional limitations and sets out to realize its new-found potentialities. Already this process is beginning to bear fruit in the emergence of a fundamentally new concept of the value and unity of human existence, in a growing insight into the increased importance and tasks of education, in the search for a more productive association of work and personality development; not least, in the phenomenal way in which the new possibilities of travel and contact among peoples are beginning to be utilized. Resistance to these tendencies cannot continue indefinitely. No political system can escape their operation. Unmistakably, the peoples of the world are beginning to respond to the feeling that in spite of every obstacle they are in the process of bringing about the unity of mankind.

But this unity must on no account be conceived in an indiscriminate and mechanical fashion. Having developed so far within the bounds of particular civilizations and nations, mankind owes all that it values most highly to its formation under specific national and cultural influences. It is from these national and cultural roots that men draw their strength. They lose these invaluable assets if they are uprooted and indiscriminately mixed together under conditions that tend to discredit any manifestation of national individuality. The new era in human development can take a really beneficial course only if man retains his consciousness of diversity and recognizes that his true wealth lies precisely in this diversity and variety, in a responsible interplay among the various branches of mankind. Mankind is the many-colored spectrum of the rainbow, not the dismal gray that results when all colors are mixed together. It is the melody that can arise only from the interplay of all its separate tones.

To learn to perceive the unity of mankind amid the multiplicity and variety of its civilizations and their organic interplay is the great task and the great problem of our time. If we can meet this challenge, we can overcome even the most serious political divisions and conflicts. But it will be possible only if we refuse to be diverted from this great universal view and get bogged down by small questions, if we try instead to resolve the questions of detail on the basis of the general view—if we try, in other words, to go *with* the general movement of man's development, not against it. The peoples of the West, with their rich and largely unexploited heritage, have every right to look toward the future with good hope if only they remain faithful to what is best in their own inheritance.

Over and above the great problems that pertain to mankind as a whole, we are still faced with numerous problems on the national level. With the immense complication of the material and intellectual apparatus of our existence, the states, too, have fallen heir to a multitude of new tasks, especially as regards the problem of state and society. There is hardly a field in which the contemporary Western outlook is so full of contradictions, and in which clarification is more urgently needed.

There is, however, no use in trying to master such problems with the methods of traditional statecraft, however justified a place these methods still have in the over-all picture. Such honored concepts as that of the "separation of powers" still have their value, but by themselves they are wholly inadequate to the great problems of our time. The latter can be mastered only through a concrete appreciation of the whole tremendous process in which we are involved, through a conscious association with it. In our dynamic era, we can no longer think in terms of a mechanical, static stabilization. The dynamism itself must become the basis of any stabilization.

Furthermore, the power problems of our era are by no means the responsibility of governments alone. These problems are so new, so complex, and so overwhelming that their solution is imaginable only on the basis of long-range, comprehensive, and extremely flexible political action. And no government can attempt such action with any hope of success unless it possesses a firm support for its policy in the nation at large. Such a policy thus presupposes an attitude of conscious responsibility not only on the part of the leaders but on that of the masses as well.

Nor is this by any means the only burden laid upon the individual by the increase of power in our era. The general, public power problems represent only one side of power, the political side. Beside them stand the mass of private power relationships and their problems involving individuals, firms, groups, and societies. Here the role of politics must be limited to maintaining an outward stability until such time as it can be undergirded by an inner stability. The creation of this inner stability is a matter for individuals. What it requires is the education—or self-education— of individuals to the degree of public awareness needed to confront these tremendously increased power problems.

RESPONSIBILITY AND INSIGHT

The counterpart of power is responsibility. Just as every individual has power, every individual has responsibility. The control of power in the industrial age is by no means just a matter of assigning responsibility to the appropriate control organs. Still less is it a matter of that favorite panacea of our time, the creation of new institutions. At bottom, it is a question of creating a new spirit of responsibility, an immensely heightened consciousness of the nature and extent of our power and of our responsibility for it. The general increase of power in the industrial era implies a correspondingly general distribution of responsibility. Without such a spirit of responsibility, raised to the height of our power itself, all institutions would remain mere empty forms.

And what, precisely, do we mean by responsibility? Basically, responsibility for the individual means the same thing that Christianity means by guilt and humility—only in a broader sense that can be understood and accepted even by those who do not belong in spirit to the Christian community. (For the non-Western peoples, the appeal of Christianity has been impaired by its identification with colonialism.) It is the Christian question "Who is thy neighbor?" applied in the most generalized fashion to all mankind.

But for such responsibility to be genuine and efficacious, it is necessary not only that the will which animates it be genuine but that it be united with a corresponding insight. And we have already seen that such political insight is extraordinarily difficult to achieve, since its basic presuppositions are directly in conflict with the conditions of the industrial age. A genuine insight must be comprehensive and capable of penetrating to the fundamentals; whereas the problems of power in the industrial age are diffuse, complex, and largely concealed. The concept of insight, moreover, includes an insight into the limits of power, the limits which man himself must impose on his own power—for example, an appreciation of the fact that man is not a material but a person and, as such, requires special protection.

How, then, are men and institutions to be imbued with such a spirit of responsibility? The question will not be resolved by any mere demonstration or preaching of the need for responsibility. In principle, this is nowhere contested; indeed, it is ceaselessly asserted on all sides. Yet the prevalence of these appeals to responsibility does not mean that they are taken seriously. Indeed, for the individual of today, education or self-education to public responsibility seems an almost hopeless undertaking. He stands as a tiny cog in an immense machine that he is quite incapable of seeing or understanding as a whole. Hence the feeling of impotence in face of the unchained flood of events that besets the very people who are predisposed by nature to be most acutely conscious of their responsibility.

Against all such temptations, one can at least try to keep the spirit of responsibility alive in oneself. But the more clearly one realizes one's own weakness, the more understandably will one hesitate to preach responsibility to others. The more unrestrainedly the spirit of responsibility is invoked and laid claim to on every side, the more one runs the risk not merely of being misunderstood but of becoming laughable and accomplishing the opposite of what one intends.

Decisive as is the spirit of responsibility in our time, therefore, it is just as impossible to determine how genuine and widespread it is, or to do much about it. One can only hope. To the extent that it is genuine, however, a good deal can undoubtedly be done to promote this spirit of responsibility indirectly and open up ways for it to become active and prove itself.

If we really wish to encourage a responsible attitude that does justice to the continuous growth of power in our time, one of our most urgent tasks is to reorient our education from its present role as a preparation for certain static forms of life, whether traditional or rational, and redirect it toward the inculcation of a spirit of dynamic responsibility. In principle, this shift of emphasis occurred with the shift to political democracy—but only in principle. As we see every day, the spirit of democracy is still very ambiguous and has in no sense fully established itself. Democracy still represents a task rather than an achievement. Education, which now amounts to a kind of commercial transaction aimed at private cultivation and the specialized development of the individual, needs to return to its original public function—for the sake of man himself as well as for the sake of his role in maintaining the industrial civilization.

What other modes of action are available to governments and individuals, and within a useful period of time? What we need is not the establishment of maximum programs but of minimum ones: a listing of those immediate tasks that really come to grips with the problem and can be carried through with a minimum of controversy and within a limited period.

The Rediscovery of Tension

Among the most obvious of these requirements is a fresh approach to the intellectual analysis of man's situation in the industrial era. Recovery of the intellectual control which has been so largely surrendered in the course of the last hundred years is the indispensable basis for that deeper insight into the nature of power and its problems without which no true spirit of responsibility can fruitfully develop. Instead of reaffirming the laissez-faire spirit that governs our production of knowledge and has led to an ever-increasing intellectual chaos, we must make a conscious effort to resynthesize our knowledge with such clarity and lucidity that the concrete tasks to be undertaken can be intelligently defined. Only on the basis of such a total view can the relevant questions really be seen and realistically posed in their true perspectives.

The lack of comprehensive knowledge of our era has been one of its most fundamental weaknesses. This deficiency reflects not only the overwhelming nature of the developments we have experienced, but also our persistent inclination to try to grasp them in ways that suited the past or suit the formal requirements of the existing branches of knowledge. The result is the radical division of our knowledge between the "scientific" and the political or humanistic.

Here, too, our task is not simply to complete the previous development but to adjust ourselves to a wholly new situation. The division must be overcome by a form of continuing synthesis that avoids getting stuck in the mass of data but is nevertheless rooted in a real understanding of the basic lines worked out by specialized investigation. In view of the established orientation of our thinking toward the existing professional fields, this will require a special exertion—but one that, in addition to being politically indispensable, should also be of the greatest value to science and scholarship by reason of the increased pressure for intellectual clarification and awareness that will result from it. Moreover, this new synthesis must be approached not as a one-time procedure but as a continuous process, no less continuous than the actual broadening of our knowledge.

We are, in particular, confronted by two tasks of fundamental significance for which points of departure and materials are already available and which can therefore be carried out at least in initial outline within a reasonable time.

The first and most fundamental is the attempt to gain a general perspective over the whole development of mankind. All policy that is directed beyond the immediate present requires such a general view. Only on the basis of such a general perspective can the conflicts between West and East, North and South be seen as a whole and brought to a solution. The materials for such an undertaking have accumulated in great quantities in recent decades. What have been lacking are the penetrating insights needed to bring this overwhelming mass of material into a usable configuration. For this we need a radically new departure.

The second task, which is the counterpart of the first, is the recovery of a general view of the over-all state of our present systematic knowledge. The development and increasing specialization of science and scholarship in the last decades have swollen our knowledge to monstrous proportions. The means available for synthesizing it do not even suffice to ensure its immediate, practical use. They are wholly insufficient to reduce it to a more generally usable form in which we would have it available for the great decisions that confront us. So far, this problem has scarcely been perceived, still less attacked.

The normal processes of interdisciplinary discussion are in no way sufficient for such an endeavor. Here, too, we are faced with the need for a radically new approach rather than merely an improvement of existing methods. Our knowledge, for example, cannot usefully be synthesized *encyclopedically*, but neither is there any use in trying to synthesize it *methodologically*. Methods attack their objects only from without; this task can only be attempted from within.

There is, however, an alternative procedure far better suited to the nature of the task. By taking as our point of departure certain basic *structural relationships* encountered in the different fields of knowledge, we can make an attempt to reduce these structural relationships to a common denominator. If we thus succeed in establishing a common foundation, it should not be too difficult to hold together by this means an absolutely unlimited mass of detailed findings.

The structural relationship of *tension* offers itself as a point of departure for such a new synthesis developed from the ground upward. Tension is found as the basic structure throughout all the fields known to us, from the structure of the atom up to that of the various civilizations. Man's whole existence is a network of tensions. We see this in his physical existence in the rhythm of the "ages of man" and the years. All his cultural achievements spring from the overcoming of the tension between feeling and understanding, as we can see in the life and work of the great cultural creators. The tensions which have been mastered in their works speak to us, and what we gain from these works arises from our capacity to let these tensions vibrate within us once again.

All man's greatest political, military, and social achievements reflect the overcoming of tension. As Jacob Burckhardt wrote in his *Observations on World History*, "The destiny of peoples and states, the direction of whole civilizations may depend on the ability of an extraordinary man to hold out under extreme spirit-

ual tensions and exertions at certain critical times. The whole subsequent history of Middle Europe has been conditioned by the
fact that Frederick the Great was supremely capable of doing this
from 1759 to 1763." Such tensions have a twofold significance in
a man's life, in the achievements to which they impel him and in
the growth of spiritual energies that comes to him from their successful mastery. In Nietzsche's words, "What does not destroy me
makes me stronger."

Above all, the relationship of man to himself is a tension between his animal basis and his "higher" self—between his original,
"natural" state and the destiny that constitutes him as a person.
It is quite wrong to view man's bondage to his body as nothing
but a regrettable animal inheritance that must be overcome to the
advantage of pure reason. Man's most valuable impulses and
forces, including the impulse toward rationality itself, arise precisely from this animal heritage. Man is not *primarily* a rational
being; he merely achieves what is at best a partial, limited rationality in the course of his development. The natural tendency of
this development is toward a heightened dynamic balance or tension between the irrational and rational forces in his endowment.
While this equilibrium was particularly characteristic of the
Greeks, the whole civilization of the agricultural age rested on
a relatively well-balanced equilibrium of irrational and rational
forces. As we have already suggested, the overweighting of the
balance on the side of rationality in the industrial age has not
only aggravated our inability to control power but has led to an
impoverishment of the spiritual forces of our whole civilization.

We have also spoken of the underlying tension in Western
civilization between the concept of self-realization or self-development that originated in the Greek tradition and the impulse
toward self-conquest or self-mastery that finds its highest expression in the Biblical tradition and in Christianity. (Religion, so
often defined in terms of man's relationship to God, can perhaps
be even better defined in terms of man's relationship to Nature—
including his own nature.) The latent opposition between self-

conquest and self-realization is encountered once again in the contrast between Hegel's stress on the overcoming of man's animal origins and Marx's insistence on his development as an integral part of nature.

Here again, however, the balance in our own time has tipped in such a way that the tension itself has been disturbed. While Communism loudly reiterates the most narrowly materialistic doctrine of self-development, the West appears to have forgotten its alternative tradition and to be ready to proclaim a similar materialistic doctrine with almost equal fervor. Yet it is only through a reaffirmation of the principle of self-conquest that we can hope to grapple successfully with our growing power problem. If we are to see the problems of our time only in terms of production and the organization it entails, there is really no basic contradiction between the West and Communism. With both sides restricting their allegiance to a mere principle of self-development, the East-West conflict would be nothing more than a gigantic world-historical misunderstanding. The opposition between East and West makes sense only when it is grasped at its root, in the dichotomy between self-conquest and self-fulfillment. And, if we do so grasp it, we also open up—in principle—the possibility of getting into a dialogue about it. For we are, after all, concerned not merely with averting a catastrophe but, beyond this, with finding the basis for enduring coexistence.

In addition to its derangement of some of the tensions most characteristic of man's past experience, the industrial age has strongly tended to devalue the idea of tension itself. In earlier periods, tension in the sense in which it is here discussed was recognized in the civilizations of both East and West. In the West, however, the concept of tension has been increasingly thrust aside and discredited in the course of the industrial revolution. The simple, obvious forms of tension between man and nature seem to be more and more suspended in our artificial world. The increasing complication of the structure of industrial civilization has produced a state of affairs in which, instead of being subjected to a comparatively few tensions that he could digest and make fruitful for his inner growth, man is assailed and torn apart by a multitude of tensions. Indeed, man's life in the industrial world is nothing but a perpetual harassment by these tensions, whose natural consequence is the prevalence of heart ailments, nervous breakdowns, and other familiar ills.

At the same time, the idea of tension has shown itself to be in radical conflict with the whole intellectual structure of the industrial civilization. That civilization, as we have seen, is built up on a rectilinear principle, on processes of a straightforward rationality which are concerned with the mass production of identical products and which seek to exclude so far as possible the risks that are inherent in every tension. The result has been a radical debasement in our attitude toward tension that resembles the similar debasement in our attitude toward power. Just as the man of the industrial era fails to distinguish between the beneficent and the harmful effects of power—which itself indicates an inner tension—he also fails to distinguish between spiritually fruitful and destructive tensions. For all tensions are painful, even the fruitful ones.

Thus the civilization of the industrial age inclines so far as possible to eliminate tension altogether. Its ideal, unspoken or expressed, is a tension-free world of frictionless processes. "As soon as the Communist form of society has been established throughout the world"; "As soon as the Communist danger has been overcome"; "As soon as colonialism and its consequences are done away with"; "As soon as the United Nations achieves unconditional authority"—then, according to the common hope, tensions will at one blow be forever eliminated. Political decisions can be reduced to the mere adjustment of spheres of responsibility and the "administration of things."

This attitude, however, runs directly counter not only to foreseeable reality but to the objective necessities of our development. As it develops, our industrial civilization automatically creates ever more and ever greater power; and with this ever-increasing power it also creates ever-new tensions between this power and its control by man. Though man can and must overcome this tension again and again, he can do this only for the particular case, not once for all. Having accomplished it in one concrete case—in disarmament, for instance—he will immediately find himself confronted again with new growths of power and new tensions.

The fact is that at the level of power we have attained in the industrial era, the development of our knowledge and our power takes the form of a chain reaction, one that cannot be broken but must lead to an ever-renewed series of tensions between this power on one side and our sense of responsibility and insight on the other. This is the necessary condition of the further development of human existence. We thus are faced with a permanent necessity of mastering this continually renewed series of tensions through continually new decisions. This state of a constantly renewed tension between man and his power, between his power and its mastery, represents the basic structure of the industrial stage. Far from being able to eliminate tension in the industrial stage, we must recognize it as the structural basis of all future existence. All future existence will have to reckon not only with tensions but with greater, deeper, more complex tensions.

The consequence is that as with power, so with tension we must undertake a radical reorientation in relation to what have hitherto been the dominant tendencies of our time. We must learn to recognize tension as an unavoidable, necessary element of our existence. Instead of regarding it as an unavoidable evil, we must learn to distinguish between those tensions that are necessary and those that are in fact avoidable. And we must learn to see the necessary tensions in their positive meaning: not as mere inescapable evils but as sources of strength, the most turbulent but, for that very reason, the most life-giving sources we possess. Finally, we must once again learn to understand correctly the role of tensions in our spiritual development, and to deal with them in such a way that we shall be able to draw upon these inborn sources of strength to the very utmost.